Rain Forests
of the
World

Volume 2
Biomass–Clear-Cutting

MARSHALL CAVENDISH
NEW YORK • LONDON • TORONTO • SYDNEY

Marshall Cavendish
99 White Plains Road
Tarrytown, New York
10591-9001

www.marshallcavendish.com

Consulting Editors: Rolf E. Johnson, Nathan E. Kraucunas

Contributing Authors: Theresa Greenaway, Jill Bailey, Michael Chinery, Malcolm Penny, Mike Linley, Philip Steele, Chris Oxlade, Ken Preston-Mafham, Rod Preston-Mafham, Clare Oliver

Discovery Books
     Managing Editor: Paul Humphrey
     Project Editor: Gianna Williams
     Text Editor: Valerie Weber
     Designer: Ian Winton
     Cartographer: Stefan Chabluk
     Illustrators: Jim Channell, Stuart Lafford, Christian Webb

Marshall Cavendish
     Editor: Marian Armstrong
     Editorial Director: Paul Bernabeo

(cover) macaw

Editor's Note: Many systems of dating have been used by different cultures throughout history. *Rain Forests of the World* uses B.C.E. (Before Common Era) and C.E. (Common Era) instead of B.C. (Before Christ) and A.D. (Anno Domini, "In the Year of Our Lord") out of respect for the diversity of the world's peoples.

The publishers would like to thank the following for their permission to reproduce photographs:
52 Luiz Claudio Marigo/Bruce Coleman, 54 Weiss/Jerrican/Science Photo Library, 55 Dr. J. A. L. Cooke/Oxford Scientific Films, 56 Michael Fogden/Oxford Scientific Films, 57 Steve Turner/Oxford Scientific Films, 58 T. Whittaker/FLPA, 59 Morten Strange/NHPA, 60 Alain Compost/ Bruce Coleman, 61 Michael Fogden/ Oxford Scientific Films, 62 Dave Watts/NHPA, 63 Bruce Beehler/NHPA, 64 Luiz Claudio Marigo/Bruce Coleman, 65 Kim Taylor/Bruce Coleman, 66 Kathie Atkinson/Oxford Scientific Films, 67 Lynwood Chace/FLPA, 68 David M. Dennis/Oxford Scientific Films, 69 Stephen Dalton/NHPA, 70 Dr. Rod Preston-Mafham/ Premaphotos Wildlife, 71 Ken Preston-Mafham/Premaphotos Wildlife, 72 Gerald Thompson/Oxford Scientific Films, 73 Richard Davies/Oxford Scientific Films, 74 Michael Fogden/Bruce Coleman, 75 Michael Fogden/Oxford Scientific Films, 76-77 Fred Hoogervorst/Foto Natura/FLPA, 77 Eric Soder/NHPA, 78 Martin Wendler/NHPA, 79 Silvestris/ FLPA, 81 Morten Strange/NHPA, 82 Terry Whittaker/FLPA, 83 Luiz Claudio Marigo/Bruce Coleman, 85 T. Montford/Foto Natura/ FLPA, 86 Gerard Lacz/FLPA, 88 Jurgen & Christine Sohns/FLPA, 89 Jane Burton/Bruce Coleman, 90 Belinda Wright/Oxford Scientific Films, 91 Michael Sewell/ Oxford Scientific Films, 92 G. I. Bernard/NHPA, 93 Gunter Ziesler/Bruce Coleman, 94 Silvestris/FLPA, 95 T. Whittaker/ FLPA, 96 Mark Newman/FLPA, 97 Harold Taylor Abipp/Oxford Scientific Films, 98 George Bernard/Oxford Scientific Films, 99 Ken Preston-Mafham/Premaphotos Wildlife, 101 Edward Parker/Oxford Scientific Films, 102 Stephen Downer/Oxford Scientific Films, 103 Bruce Coleman, 104 Martyn Colbeck/Oxford Scientific Films, 105 Silvestris/FLPA, 106 Phil Devries/Oxford Scientific Films, 107 Morten Strange/NHPA, 108 F Hoogervorst/Foto Natura/FLPA, 109 Lake County Museum/Corbis

Library of Congress Cataloging-in-Publication Data
Rain forests of the world.
                          p. cm.
           Includes bibliographical references and index.
           Contents: v. 1. Africa-bioluminescence — v. 2. Biomass-clear-cutting — v. 3. Climate and weather-emergent — v. 4. Endangered species-food web — v. 5. Forest fire-iguana — v. 6. Indonesia-manatee — v. 7. Mangrove forest-orangutan — v. 8. Orchid-red panda — v. 9. Reforestation-spider — v. 10. Squirrel-Yanomami people — v. 11. Index.
                ISBN 0-7614-7254-1 (set)
                1. Rain forests — Encyclopedias.   I.. Marshall Cavendish Corporation.
           QH86 .R39 2002
           578.734—dc21
                                                                                        2001028460

     ISBN 0-7614-7254-1 (set)
     ISBN 0-7614-7256-8 (vol. 2)

Printed and bound in Italy

07 06 05 04 03 02   6 5 4 3 2 1

Contents

The world's rain forests support enormous quantities of animal and plant life. It is useful for scientists to have a way of measuring the quantity of living, biological material, which they call biomass, that a given area of rain forest contains. Biomass includes all the plants, animals, and other organisms, such as bacteria, in an ecosystem. The measurements enable scientists to compare one part of a rain forest environment with another or compare rain forests with other environments such as prairies or deserts. Measuring biomass is also useful for discovering information about food chains and for monitoring how an ecosystem is changing from month to month or from year to year.

Biomass is normally measured as the mass of living matter in a certain area in units of metric tons per hectare or kilograms per square meter. Biomass is sometimes calculated by an entire ecosystem, such as an individual tree or a forest, rather than by hectare or square meter.

Different types of biomass can be measured. For example community biomass measures the total biomass of a community, which is a collection of animals, plants, fungi, and bacteria that live together in an area or habitat. Species biomass measures the biomass of one particular species of organism in a community.

KEY FACTS

● Biomass is the mass of living matter in a certain area of an ecosystem.

● A typical rain forest has a biomass of between 180 and 300 tn. per acre (400 and 700 metric tons per hectare). This is much higher than any other ecosystem.

● If an area of rain forest is cut down, burned, and then allowed to regrow, the biomass may never return to its original level.

These biologists are collecting leaf litter from an area of rain forest floor. They will weigh it to work out how much litter has been produced by the trees over a period of time.

Calculating Biomass

The best and most accurate calculation of biomass is called dry biomass. To do this exactly requires collecting all the living matter in an ecosystem, drying it in an oven to remove any water content, then weighing it. In the rain forest this is not possible since it would mean killing many plants and animals and cutting down huge rain forest trees.

Biomass and Farming

The increase in biomass from plant growth in a year is called net primary production. In a rain forest, net primary production is typically between 9 and 13 tn. per acre (20 and 30 metric tons per hectare) per year. In contrast slash-and-burn farmers in the rain forest can grow just 3 tn. per acre (6 metric tons per hectare) per year. Rain forests cover about 5 percent of the earth's surface but produce more than a quarter of the earth's new biomass every year.

Instead several small areas within an ecosystem are chosen at random, measured, and marked out. Then scientists take samples of plants from each area for drying and weighing. They also count the total number of plants in the area. The number of plants is multiplied by the weight of the sample plants to give an estimate of the dry biomass of the area. The populations of different animal species are also estimated to calculate the biomass of animals. The results of both plant and animal calculations are used to obtain the total biomass of the ecosystem. The biomass for a temperate rain forest might range from 65 to 130 tons per acre (150 to 300 metric tons per hectare), while a prairie biomass would be very low, less than 5 tons per acre (10 metric tons per hectare).

Biomass in Pyramids
To show the link between biomass and the plants and animals in a particular rain forest food chain, a diagram called a pyramid of biomass is used. This shows the biomass of the plants and animals at each level of the food chain.

In most ecosystems green plants make up the majority of the total biomass and so form the largest section of the biomass pyramid. The proportion of the total biomass made up by plants is higher in tropical rain forests than in any other ecosystem.

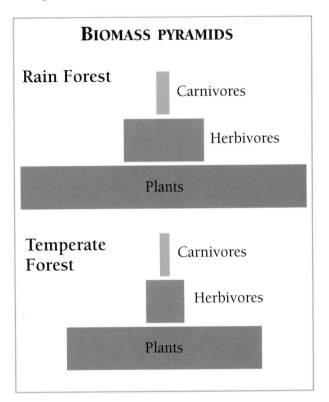

BIOMASS PYRAMIDS

Constant Biomass
The biomass of an ecosystem can go up and down. For example in a deciduous forest, biomass rises in the spring and summer as new leaves, flowers, and fruits grow, and biomass drops in the autumn as they fall. However, in a rain forest, biomass stays fairly constant year-round. The creation of new biomass by rain forest plants (called producers) and growing animals is balanced by loss of biomass, caused by animals (called consumers) eating the plants, by leaves falling and decaying, and by plants and animals dying.

Check these out:
● Carbon Cycle ● Ecosystem ● Food Web

Biotechnology

Tomato plants that produce tastier tomatoes can be made by adding new genes to the original plants. Some animals can be exactly copied, or cloned, by replacing the genes in an animal's egg with genes from the animal to be copied. Both of these are examples of biotechnology at work.

Biotechnology is used to increase plant and animal food production, to diagnose disease, improve medical treatments, produce new drugs, and to help dispose of industrial wastes. Biotechnologists normally work with animal or plant cells, the genetic material inside cells, and with microorganisms, organisms so small they can only be seen with a microscope. Microorganisms are essential in biotechnology because they reproduce and grow much more quickly than animals and plants. Using cell division, one cell can multiply into millions in just a few days. Thus useful microorganisms can be grown on a large scale.

Genetic Engineering

The most well-known branch of biotechnology is genetic engineering. In the nuclei (the tiny oval center) of all cells are microscopically small chemical structures called chromosomes. Each chromosome in a cell is made up of many sections called genes, which control one or more characteristics of the organism, such as eye color in humans. Chromosomes and genes are called genetic material.

A scientist examines seedlings grown from seeds that have been genetically engineered. The characteristics of the seedlings will differ from those of the parent plants.

54

Genetic engineering means altering the genetic, or hereditary, material of a cell, usually by selecting genes from a cell of one species of organism and adding them to a cell of another species. This causes the characteristics of the first organism to appear in the second.

Genetic engineering has many applications. One example is the development of genetically modified (GM) crops. Genes from one species of plant are put into the chromosomes of another, creating crops that can, for example, grow larger than they could before, or that are resistant to particular diseases.

The Rain Forest Gene Pool

The world's rain forests contain millions of different species of animals, plants, and microorganisms. Every single one of these species carries its own unique set of genes. Thus there are millions of genes, called a gene pool, that could be useful for creating new medicines, crops that are resistant to disease and cold, and new chemicals for industry.

With all these genes, the rain forest is an enormous and precious resource for biotechnology. One of the most famous examples of a rain forest species being used for the benefit of humanity is the rosy periwinkle, found in Madagascar. This small plant produces two powerful chemicals, vinblastine and

vincristine, that are used to treat two different kinds of cancer.

With the loss of rain forests comes the loss of many species and their genes. Biotechnology could also help to save the rain forests themselves if it could create high-yield or disease-resistant crops or food-producing

IN FOCUS

Wild Crops to the Rescue

All the world's crops were originally wild plants. The cacao (ku-KOW) tree, from which chocolate and cocoa come, is grown mostly in Africa but originated in South American rain forests. To improve the yield from the trees and their resistance to disease, growers are taking genes from wild cacao trees in the rain forest to add to their own domesticated species.

microorganisms that would reduce the need for cutting down forests to develop the land for farming.

Check these out:
● Biodiversity ● Conservation ● Disease
● Exploitation ● Medicinal Plant

Bird

The rain forests of the world abound with birds of just about every shape, size, and color. At least 2,500 species of birds live in the tropical rain forests—a third of all known species in the world. Why? Food is abundant, the habitat is complex, and there is no extreme winter season.

The rain forest is the richest biome on earth. (A biome is a large geographic region made up of distinctive plant and animal communities.) The rain forest provides a wide range of fruits, seeds, and nectar-rich flowers for hungry birds to eat. Swarms of insects feed on the leaves or burrow in the ground; they too are food for birds. Other birds eat reptiles and small mammals that forage on the forest floor or high in the trees. At the top of the food chain are large predators like owls and eagles.

Because there is no cold season in the Tropics, birds don't need to change their feeding habits as the year passes the way birds do in other climatic zones. This means that more species can live together in the same area, each with its own diet. Some feed on nectar year-round, like hummingbirds in the Americas or sunbirds, which resemble hummingbirds, in Africa and Asia. Other birds eat only fruits or seeds, and insect eaters abound. With its many layers in the canopy, the complex structure of the rain forest increases the number of ecological niches, areas with specific conditions that could suit specific animals, and therefore increases the number of species that can live there.

A saber-wing hummingbird feeding in Costa Rica. As it collects nectar from the flower, it also picks up pollen grains.

56

Nectar Eaters and Pollinators

Flowers produce sweet nectar to attract birds, butterflies, and other insects, as well as bats, mice, and even fish, to pollinate them. Birds that feed on nectar usually have long, slender beaks for probing into flowers to reach the nectaries, most often found at the bases of the petals. Sunbirds and hummingbirds are good examples of nectar eaters. In the rain forests of Australia and New Guinea, honey eaters have brushlike tongues to help them extract nectar.

All of these nectar feeders also pollinate the flowers. Bird-pollinated flowers are often tubular so the bird must poke its head inside and brush past the stamens before it can reach the nectar. It emerges dusted with pollen. This pollination system works well because when a bird finds a flower with a good supply of nectar, it looks for other flowers of the same species for its next drink. A few birds "cheat" by pecking through the base of a flower to get at the nectar from the outside. The result is that the flower is robbed of its nectar without being pollinated. To make up for this possibility, bird-pollinated plants usually have many flowers to ensure that at least some become pollinated.

Fruit Eaters and Seed Dispersers

Many species of fruit-eating birds flourish in the rain forest. Most help the plants they feed on by scattering their seeds. The largest group of fruit-eating birds is the pigeon, many of which are very brightly colored. Pigeons swallow fruits whole. After the flesh has been removed in the bird's crop, which is a pouch near the bottom of a bird's throat where its food is prepared for digestion, the seeds

IN FOCUS

Charging Cassowaries

Cassowaries (KA-suh-wer-ees), a group of fruit-eating birds that occasionally also consume insects and small mammals, live only in the rain forest. They are flightless and nearly 5 ft. (1.5 m) tall. Highly adapted to forest life, they inhabit northern Australia and the islands around New Guinea. Their long, coarse plumage looks more like hair than feathers, acting as armor when they push through the thorny undergrowth. The hard crest on their head, called a casque, works like a crash helmet. They need this protection because they can run at up to 30 mi. (48 km) per hour through the thickest vegetation. Brightly colored skin covers their head and neck, sometimes with hanging wattles. Cassowaries are very dangerous to humans if they are cornered, kicking with sharp claws as they jump at the enemy feetfirst.

A black—headed caique, a small parrot from Central America, slices up fruits held in its claw with its sharp beak.

pass through its digestive system intact. The seeds then drop, often far from the original plant. Parrots hold the fruit in one claw and remove the flesh with their sharp, scissorlike beaks, then drop the seed on the forest floor.

Other birds regurgitate the seed after swallowing it. A few birds, like some woodpeckers, bury seeds for eating later; forgotten seeds will grow in the place where they were buried. Because fruit is such a rich source of food, some fruit-eating birds can gather all they need very quickly, leaving them with time to spare for complex courting and nesting behaviors.

Birds like finches crunch up seeds rather than swallowing them whole.

Plants whose seeds are eaten in this way often have fruits that are "wasteful," so that when a bird pecks at a seed, other seeds fall out and drift away or float down a stream, landing at a distance from the parent plant and thus spreading the species. Other plants have poisonous seeds so birds won't eat them in the first place. These seeds often have sticky or spiny coats that stick to the feathers of passing birds and thus are distributed by "air mail."

Insect Hunters
Birds do not feed only on rain forest plants. Many also eat rain forest animals, especially insects. Insects crowd the topmost leaves and clumps of hanging moss on tree branches that are regularly visited by birds such as warblers and flycatchers. Warblers use their short,

slender beaks to pick insects from among leaves, often so high up that the birds are hard to see from the ground. Flycatchers take their food on the wing, making short flights from a perch. They have wide beaks, often with bristles around the edges that work like a net to guide their prey into their mouths.

Some birds feed from tiny ponds in trees. Bromeliads (broe-MEE-lee-ads)—sometimes called wild pines because the leaves look like those found on pineapples—grow on the higher branches of rain forest trees, their cupped leaves filled with water. These pools have their own populations of insect larvae and frogs. In the forests of Jamaica, a very specialized predatory bird, called the wild pine sergeant, feeds on the life in these tiny pools.

Farther down the tree trunks, woodpeckers dig for beetle grubs, while woodcreepers and wood hoopoes (HOO-poos) probe cracks in the bark to extract spiders and insect larvae. On the ground, antbirds and ant thrushes feed on the huge columns of ants marching across the forest floor. Soldier ants kill even quite large insects; where

A crimson–winged woodpecker from Malaysia digs for grubs. Even small dead twigs can contain grubs that woodpeckers will eat.

they are hunting, grasshoppers and cockroaches are always trying to escape. Some antbirds specialize in catching these insects rather than the ants themselves. Other birds, like the large family of pittas, hunt through the leaf litter finding large insects for themselves.

Butterflies often gather on the ground where an animal has urinated because they need the extra nitrogen to help form their eggs. Many different species of birds feed on the groups of butterflies, avoiding some that are brightly colored, which indicates that they might be poisonous. Many also eat the caterpillars.

IN FOCUS

Ghost in the Forest

The huge milky eagle owl (or Verreaux's eagle owl) is found only in the deepest forests of Africa. It is rarely seen, but it has a loud, haunting cry, which has given rise to many legends and superstitions among forest dwellers. People sometimes think it is the spirit of a dead ancestor or some other unearthly being.

Other Forest Hunters

Toward the top of the food chain, hawks and owls feed on frogs, lizards, snakes, other birds, and mammals. Some of these predatory forest birds are enormous. The eagle owl in Asia and the great gray owl in North America's temperate rain forests are huge birds, feeding mainly by day, unlike most other owls. Their main prey are rodents that scour the forest floor for dropped seeds and large insects.

Forest eagles are usually also big, like the crowned eagle in Africa, the monkey-eating eagle in Asia, and the harpy eagle, which inhabits an area from southern Mexico to northern Argentina. While many small forest hawks and owls haunt the woods, there's a place in every forest for a large predator hunting over a wide territory, able to take large prey.

Forest Nests

As well as food, the forest provides plenty of nesting material, such as plant fibers and dead leaves, plus moss for lining the

A newly hatched maleo chick digs its way to the surface. It is independent from the moment it hatches, needing no help from its parents.

nest. Many birds use spiders' webs to bind their nests together, sometimes collecting it at great risk as they hover in front of the sticky webs that can be big enough to trap an unwary bird.

An unusual group of forest birds are the mound builders, or megapodes (meaning "big-feet" in Latin), found in Australia and Southeast Asia. They dig large pits, which they fill with vegetation, lay their eggs on top, and then cover the eggs with sand or soil. As the vegetation rots, it gives off enough heat to incubate the eggs. The maleo, which lives on the island of Sulawesi in Indonesia, does not use vegetation; it lays its eggs in piles of sand beside hot springs or near hot volcanic gases bubbling from the ground.

Dead and hollow trees, both standing and lying on the forest floor, furnish nesting places—something often overlooked by people wanting to "improve" forest land by removing all dead and dying material. Parrots and woodpeckers dig out holes in the dead wood; when they have finished with the hollow trees, their nesting holes are used by a wide variety of other birds or animals.

IN FOCUS

The Quetzal

The quetzal (ket-SAHL), the sacred bird of the Maya people, eats wild avocado fruits by hovering beside a branch and tearing the fruit off in its wide beak. After flying away, it removes the flesh of the fruit and spits the seed out on the ground. In doing this it plants food trees in the forest for its descendants.

Courting in the Dark

The rain forest provides birds with plenty of food and nesting places, but it's not without problems, one of which is poor visibility. High in the canopy, light abounds, but birds living lower down are in a constant green twilight. This makes it difficult for them to communicate with each other, which is especially important during the courtship season. For this reason pigeons, parrots, and many other rain forest birds are brightly colored, usually with highly contrasting plumage bearing flashes of color that show up clearly in the dim light. The red-sided parrot that lives in Australia and New Guinea takes this to an extreme; males and females are completely different colors. The male is bright green with red patches on the sides, and the female is dark red with blue patches.

Parrots also have loud voices, enabling them to keep in contact with each other in the dense forest. Some other birds make low, booming sounds that also carry a long way. The quetzal has a haunting, hooting call, and the huge eagle owl and the spotted owl produce deep, repeated calls that echo among the trees. The bellbirds of Central America are good examples of forest singers, producing a ringing duet in which male and female each has its own part.

Attracting Attention

Birds of paradise live in New Guinea and Australia. In Papua, New Guinea, alone there are 43 species, most of them about the size of a starling, around 8½ inches (22 cm) long.

Because most birds of paradise have dark plumage, they are hard to see until they begin their courting ritual, when tufts and patches of bright feathers begin to shine in the dim light. Their swaying movements, common to many courtship displays, show off their metallic sheen. Some male birds of paradise display close to the ground, while others perform high in the trees. Some hang upside down from a branch, while others wave or rattle their colorful, elongated plumes as they sway from side to side. Their calls are usually mechanical sounds, clicks and buzzes, that carry well through the forest.

Dull brown and quite inconspicuous, bowerbirds live in the same area as birds of paradise. Like other forest birds, many of them have loud, harsh voices. These birds build courtship bowers. The main bower is a small thatched hut. When it is complete, the bowerbirds collect conspicuous objects, such as flowers, fruit, beetle wings, and even bottle tops, and arrange them around the entrance in piles of matching colors or in patterns to attract a female. When such courtship bowers were first discovered in 1870, the explorers thought they had been made by local children.

Bowerbirds select decorations for their bower by color. Here a male satin bowerbird in Australia offers a female an arrangement of blue and yellow feathers.

Birds in Danger

The forest tribes in Central America have always exploited parrots. Macaws (muh-

Female birds of paradise are drab compared to the spectacular males. This male raggiana bird of paradise displays his glowing plumage to a female.

one macaw for the equivalent of a year's wages. Instead of climbing up to the nests, today people simply fell the trees, removing whatever nestlings survive the fall so that the forest is damaged as well as the bird population.

The only way to protect the birds is to stop the trade. However, as long as people are prepared to break the law and spend large sums of money to own one of these beautiful birds, that is easier said than done.

KAWS), sometimes over 3 feet (1 m) long, were the main victims. Until recently the birds were so highly valued that each nest belonged to a particular tribe. The tribe collected the fat chicks for food at about three months old, just before they left the nest, but kept one chick from each brood alive. Its tail feathers were plucked each time they grew, to be used in ceremonial costumes. When the bird could grow no more feathers, it was killed.

Since Europeans arrived in Central America, eight species of macaws have become extinct, and all the others are endangered. This was caused not by aboriginal exploitation but by the international trade in parrots as pets.

Although the birds have been legally protected since 1985, the trade is very difficult to stop; a farmer can often sell

IN FOCUS

From Brides to Black Markets

Papuans once used the feathers of birds of paradise as money to buy brides and to decorate their outfits for ceremonial dances. For centuries they hunted these birds with bows and arrows. When the world of Western fashion discovered the feathers, several species were soon threatened with extinction. In 1924 hunting birds of paradise was banned, but poachers still sometimes hunt them illegally for the black market.

Check these out:
- Communication ● Courtship ● Eagle
- Hummingbird ● Nest and Nest Building
- Owl ● Parrot, Macaw, and Parakeet
- Pollination ● Toucan ● Vulture

Bromeliad

Bromeliads (broe-MEE-lee-ads) are short plants with crownlike clusters of stiff, spiky leaves. Several hundred different kinds grow in Central and South American rain forests. Many bromeliads grow on the ground, where their spiky leaves, which can be over 6½ feet (2 m) long, form dense thickets. Others grow as epiphytes, perched on the trunks and branches of rain forest trees.

The leaf crown of a bromeliad collects rainwater in its base, which is called a tank. The leaves gradually soak up the rainwater and use it for making food by photosynthesis just like any other plant. Ground-living bromeliads get minerals from the soil, but those growing as epiphytes absorb

Brightly colored flower spikes rise from the leaf crowns of these epiphytic bromeliads in the Brazilian rain forest.

minerals from dead leaves and animal droppings trapped around their roots. Small animals that fall into the tanks and drown also provide the epiphytes with some food. The bromeliads do not take any food from the trees on which they live.

The water-filled bromeliad tanks are home to small frogs, snails, lots of mosquitoes, and many other animals. About 250 different kinds of animals have been found living in bromeliad tanks in Costa Rica alone. Some of the frogs that breed in the treetop tanks never come down to the ground. Their tadpoles browse on the microscopic green plants that grow in the tanks and also eat many of the mosquito and other insect larvae.

A variety of birds and insects pollinate the colorful flower spikes springing from the bromeliad crowns. Most bromeliads then produce juicy berries, some of which are good to eat. The leaves of some bromeliads also yield useful fibers, some of which can be woven into very fine cloth. In the Philippines fibers from pineapple leaves are used to make shirts and other clothes.

Check these out:
- Canopy ● Cockroach ● Crustacean ● Dragonfly
- Ecology ● Epiphyte ● Frog and Toad ● Plant

Bug

Some carry toxic saliva, some bite swimmers' toes, some harbor tropical diseases—bugs are a large and varied group of insects. Active year-round, rain forest bugs vary enormously in size, from tiny insects a few millimeters long to giant aquatic predators that can reach nearly 4 inches (10 cm).

Many superficially resemble beetles: both have six legs; a body divided into a head, thorax, and abdomen; and many have wings folded across the back. The main difference between beetles and bugs lies in their mouthparts: beetles have biting or chewing mouthparts, while bugs have a piercing and sucking mouthpart called a rostrum, which acts rather like a hypodermic syringe. Some bugs' rostrums are designed to be plunged into the stems of plants to suck up sap. Others, however, use their rostrum to pierce animals, either to completely suck them dry or simply to feed on some of their blood. Some of these bloodsuckers are known to feed on human blood and can carry and transmit disease. Many bugs' rostrums are so long that they are held folded backward along the underside of the insect's body.

Unlike beetles, which start off life as larvae or grubs that then change into pupae from which the adults eventually emerge, juvenile bugs, or nymphs, are very similar to their adult forms. They undergo several molts on their way to adulthood; with each molt their wing buds become more developed. However, only the adult bug has fully functional wings.

The bugs' forewings are known as hemielytra. The first two-thirds of these wings are leathery, while the last third is clear and veined; it folds away for protection when the insect rests.

KEY FACTS

● There are tens of thousands of species of bugs in rain forests.

● Their mouthparts are modified to form a tube that they use to pierce plants and other animals.

● Bugs are found in almost every type of habitat in the rain forest.

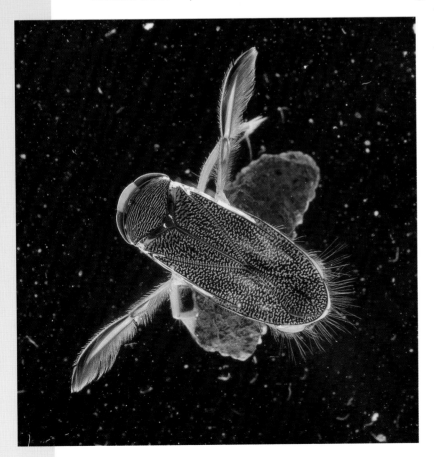

The boatman, or back swimmer, is aquatic but needs to breathe air.

On, Next to, and Away from Water

Some bugs are completely aquatic and spend their entire lives as both nymph and adult in forest pools and swamps. These tend to have relatively short antennae, and their hind legs are modified to form what look like a pair of oars for propelling the bug through the water. These bugs remain air breathers and must return to the water's surface to take in more air. Some can take down a supply of air with them, trapped as a bubble on their body.

Other bugs live beside water or on the actual surface of the water. Water-repellent hairs cover the undersides of their bodies, allowing them to exploit the surface tension of the water and to skate over it in search of prey without falling in. These too have short antennae.

The majority of bugs live on land. They typically sport long antennae and bright colors, and many have a pair of scent glands that give off a noxious liquid when the bug is threatened. It is a very effective defense, and these animals are often referred to as stinkbugs.

In the rain forest, all three types of these bugs can be found in tens of thousands of species. They live in the swamps, throughout the leaf litter on the forest floor, on tree trunks, and along branches, all the way up into the rain forest canopy.

Aquatic Bugs: Back Swimmers

Although they are aquatic, these medium-sized bugs fly well, mainly at night. They typically live upside down on the underside of the water's surface, waiting for the telltale vibrations that reveal an insect has fallen in from the canopy above. The back swimmer then pounces, seizing its prey, piercing it with its short, sharp rostrum, and completely sucking it dry. They also have toxic saliva. Back swimmers include the water boatman that prefers to live in rivers and rain forest pools that are well stocked with water plants.

Water Scorpions

Despite their name, these large, aquatic bugs are not related to real scorpions. They get their name from the fact that their front pairs of legs are modified to form a large pair of

A water scorpion seizes a tadpole and sucks it dry. The bug breathes through the long tube that stretches to the water's surface.

pincers with sharp tips that curve around to face each other in front of the bug's head, like a scorpion's. The water scorpion also has a long breathing tube, or snorkel, which protrudes from the tip of the bug's abdomen and that many people mistakenly believe to be a venomous sting.

Water scorpions normally grow to ³/₄ to 1 inch (2 to 2.5 cm) long. Although they possess wings, they do not fly. Instead, water scorpions spend most of their time sitting motionless on aquatic vegetation along rivers or oxbow lakes, waiting for something to come within range of those curved pincers. They will eat small fish, tadpoles, worms, and aquatic insects of all types.

The water stick insect is similar but much more elongated, hence the name; it can reach 3 inches (8 cm) in length. It is also well camouflaged amid the surrounding vegetation.

Giant Water Bugs

Giant water bugs are similar in appearance to water scorpions except they are much larger, reaching a length of 2 to 4 inches (5 to 10 cm), depending on the species. They possess a pair of large, compound eyes that give them excellent vision. Their front pair of legs are modified to form sharp, grasping arms.

The giant water bug's short and beaklike rostrum is used to break its prey's skin and inject saliva that digests its victim's internal tissues. It can then suck up and swallow the resulting "soup." These bugs are ambush hunters and simply wait in the aquatic vegetation for suitable prey to swim by.

Caring Males

IN FOCUS

One of the most remarkable features about giant water bugs is that the males look after the eggs. After mating, the female deposits between 100 and 150 eggs onto the back of the male, where they stick tight. The eggs take about three weeks to hatch. During this time the male often sits with his back out of the water to expose the eggs to the atmosphere. In the water he often pumps his body up and down to circulate water around the eggs.

They will tackle just about anything small enough to overpower, including fish, frogs, and other insects. Some giant water bugs are known as "toe biters" because of their habit of occasionally biting swimmers' toes.

Water Striders

These are usually small bugs with long narrow bodies, long, thin limbs, and antennae. Water striders live around the water's edge and, as their name implies, they can skate across the water's surface. Their legs are so long and fine and their bodies so light that they can spread their weight over a wide area. This means that they never break through the surface tension of the water.

Water striders feed mainly on insects that accidentally fall into the water. The vibration of these fallen insects' struggles are carried across the water's surface and picked up by the sensitive feet of the water strider.

On Land: Assassin Bugs

These large, often brightly colored bugs are active hunters. They can measure up to 1 inch (2.5 cm) in length and fly

IN FOCUS

Blood-Sucking Bugs

Often found in the leafy thatch of houses in the Amazon, the Rhodnius bug's flattened body allows it to squeeze between the roof's dried leaves. At night it descends to suck the blood of the human occupants. In doing so its body can swell to the size of a large grape. Unfortunately a bite from this insect can prove to be dangerous since it often carries a variety of diseases that can prove fatal if not treated early.

quickly. They normally inhabit vegetation where they stalk other insects. Assassin bugs have an enormous proboscis (mouthpart), and their front limbs are often modified for seizing prey.

In tropical rain forests, some members of the assassin bug family have adapted to suck blood as their food source. Their sharp proboscis works just like a hypodermic needle. They can drink their fill of blood without killing their prey.

An African assassin bug peers over a leaf in search of prey.

Check these out: ● Insect ● Invertebrate

Butterfly and Moth

Butterflies and moths are some of the biggest insects in the rain forest. Moths usually have thicker and furrier bodies and tend to be duller in color than butterflies, the most colorful insects in the rain forest. Almost all butterflies fly by day and most of the moths fly by night, but otherwise the two groups are very similar. They all belong to the large group known as Lepidoptera.

Four-Stage Life Cycle

All butterflies and moths start their lives as eggs, but the creatures that emerge from the eggs are nothing like the adult insects. Wingless caterpillars, they soon start munching their way through the surrounding leaves; in some rain forests, their droppings fall like rain. Many of these little droppings help nourish the bromeliads and other plants that perch on the trunks and branches of the rain forest trees.

Caterpillars grow quickly, and some species change their skins every two or three days. Each species of caterpillar has its own particular plant it likes to eat; if the eggs are laid on the wrong plant, the caterpillars often will die. Before laying their eggs, adult females examine the plants very carefully, "tasting" the leaves with their feet. In this way, the insects find out if the leaves are fresh, healthy, and the right kind to feed their caterpillars.

Long spines, some containing powerful poisons, often protect caterpillars. The caterpillars of some South American silk moths are clothed with poisonous spines that will cause a person to bleed heavily even if their hand just brushes against them. Others, known as guinea pig caterpillars because their long, shaggy coats make them look like miniature guinea pigs, are even more dangerous. The poison in their

KEY FACTS

● Thousands of different kinds of butterflies and moths live in the rain forest, more than in all the other habitats on Earth put together.

● The wings of butterflies and moths are covered with tiny, overlapping scales, like shingles on a roof. The scales give the wings their colors. Lepidoptera, the scientific name for butterflies and moths, means "scale-wings."

● The antennae or feelers attached to the head of butterflies and moths are important sense organs. Butterfly antennae usually have little knobs at the end, but moth antennae are usually hairlike or feathery.

The beautiful colors of this South American heliconiid butterfly are produced when light reflects off the coating of tiny scales.

hair can cause serious damage to the skin of any animal that touches them.

Caterpillars are usually fully grown within two or three weeks, and then they turn into pupae (some butterfly pupae are called chrysalids). Moth pupae are usually formed in the ground or in silken cocoons spun among the leaves and twigs, but butterfly pupae often hang from the food plants. After a week or so, new adult insects break out of the pupae. Soft and crumpled at first, their wings soon expand as the insects pump fluid into them. As soon as their wings have dried and hardened, the new adults can fly away.

Broods and Foods

Because the tropical rain forest is always warm, butterflies and moths thrive there at any time of the year, usually in huge numbers. These insects can also breed at any time, and because they grow up so quickly in the warm conditions, they can produce several broods or generations each year. Some rain forest butterflies can grow from egg to adult in just three

weeks, but many of those living in cooler parts of the world need about a year.

Butterflies and moths generally like sweet foods, and most feed on the sugary nectar produced by flowers. However, they find plenty of other foods in the rain forest. Many rain forest butterflies suck the juices of overripe fruits and drink the sap oozing from damaged tree trunks. They suck up the liquids through a slender tongue called a proboscis. Some moths have sharply pointed tongues to pierce fruit skins to reach the juices. A few moths living in the forests of Southeast Asia actually pierce the skins of people and animals and feed on their blood.

The beautiful heliconiid butterflies of the South American rain forest

IN FOCUS

The Bird Wings

Bird wing butterflies live mainly in the rain forests of Indonesia and neighboring parts of Southeast Asia. They get their name because they are so big; from a distance, they can easily be mistaken for birds. The approximately 35 species include the world's biggest butterfly—the female Queen Alexandra's bird wing from New Guinea. This rather dull brown butterfly can measure about 11 in. (28 cm) across its outstretched wings. The male is a little smaller but much more colorful, with gleaming green and turquoise wings.

feed on pollen as well as nectar. They cannot swallow the pollen grains but dribble nectar over them, which dissolves some of the food material. The butterflies then suck up the resulting solution.

A Muddy Feast

Muddy patches in the rain forest often attract huge numbers of butterflies. Though belonging to many different species, they crowd together to push their tongues into the mud. This behavior is called puddling. Nearly all the butterflies involved are males, eager to find the mineral salts that they need for their reproductive systems to work properly. The females do not generally need to gather as many mineral salts and usually stay up in the canopy where most of the flowers are found.

Bluebottle swallowtails, also called blue triangle butterflies, can be seen drinking or puddling on river banks and other damp spots all over Southeast Asia.

Deceiving Enemies

Butterflies, moths, and their caterpillars have a lot of enemies, including other insects, birds, lizards, and monkeys. However, many rain forest insects avoid capture with their amazing camouflage. Leaf butterflies look just like leaves when they are at rest; their enemies take no notice of them. Many moths rest on the forest floor and look so like the surrounding dead leaves that it is almost impossible to spot them. Glass-wing butterflies have transparent wings. You can see right through them to the leaves behind; the butterflies themselves are hardly noticed. Many caterpillars are also beautifully camouflaged, looking just like twigs or even bird droppings.

Several kinds of "back-to-front" butterflies live in the rain forests. Dark spots at the rear of their wings look like false heads when the insects are at rest. The rear-wing edges may also bear slender

The Dazzling Morphos

Morpho butterflies, famous for their shimmering blue wings, include some of the most brilliant of the rain forest butterflies. Over 100 species live in the forests of South America. Usually only the males reveal these gleaming colors, while most females are brown. The morphos feed mainly on overripe and rotting fruit. Their wings are up to 8 in. (20 cm) across and used to be very popular for making brooches and other jewelry because their colors do not fade. Many butterfly colors are produced by chemical pigments that gradually fade after the butterfly's death, but the shiny blue of the morphos is due to the structure of the scales. Microscopic ridges on the scales are arranged in such a way that they reflect only blue light.

IN FOCUS

tails or ribbons that resemble antennae. Birds are fooled when they see the false antennae waving in the breeze and attack the wrong end of the insect. The butterfly flies away, leaving the bird with just a small piece of wing.

Many large moths, including several beautiful silk moths, frighten their enemies by flashing eyelike markings when they are disturbed. The markings look like the eyes of cats or owls; although the moths are quite harmless, few predators risk continuing their attack.

Warning Colors

The world's rain forests are home to many foul-tasting and poisonous butterflies and moths. Some poisonous insects eat poisonous foods—they are immune to the toxic chemicals—and store the poisons in their bodies to use for defense. Others make the poisons in their bodies. Any bird or other predator that tries to eat one of the poisonous insects is soon sick. The insects usually advertise their unpleasant nature with bright colors or bold patterns; predators soon learn that the brightly colored insects should be avoided. Poisonous butterflies of several different kinds often share the same colors or patterns. Dozens of South American butterflies, for example, are black and yellow with cream patches. The butterflies all benefit from this arrangement because a predator has to learn only one pattern before leaving all the different, yet similarly colored, insects alone.

Many harmless butterflies and moths deceive their enemies by sharing a pattern with one or more poisonous species. Once the predators have learned that eating the bold or brightly colored insects can make them sick, they avoid the harmless ones as well. This form of trickery is called mimicry. Several species of harmless moths avoid being eaten because they resemble or mimic wasps.

Colorful Moths and Dull Butterflies

Several of the tropical silk moths rival the butterflies in both size and color, but the most colorful moths belong to a group called uraniids. These are even more dazzling than most butterflies and, unlike most moths, they fly in the daytime. They are easily mistaken for swallowtail butterflies because they have little tails on their rear wings. Swarms of uraniids periodically migrate through the South American rain forests in search of fresh food plants on which to lay their eggs.

If the uraniids are butterflylike moths, then the South American owl butterflies are mothlike butterflies. Most are dull brown, and because they fly mainly at dusk, they are often mistaken for moths or bats. Their wings are nearly 8 inches (20 cm) across. Big eyespots on the undersides of their wings resemble owls' eyes, making birds frightened of attacking the butterflies.

Although less colorful than many of its relatives, this uraniid moth from Southeast Asia could easily be mistaken for a swallowtail butterfly.

Check these out:
● Camouflage ● Insect ● Invertebrate

The tropical rain forest is a noisy place. Birdsongs, the trills, whines, and buzzes of insects, and the rustling of leaves reveal the presence of animals. But where are they? Many forest inhabitants are hard to spot.

Many rain forest animals have evolved disguises to avoid being noticed. These disguises are called camouflage. Some use camouflage to escape the prying eyes of their enemies, others use it to creep up on their prey without being seen.

KEY FACTS

● **Shadows often give away animal shapes. The back of a four-footed animal often appears lighter than its belly because the belly is in shadow. Deer and antelope have pale bellies and dark backs, making them hard to spot.**

● **In damp weather some species of frog and toad become darker to match the darker color of wet leaves and soil around them.**

Spot the Mimics

The simplest form of camouflage involves matching the color and pattern of the animal's background. When at rest, many moths and butterflies blend in with bark or leaves. Green tree frogs stay quite still, with their legs drawn close to their bodies and their eyelids closed to hide their large eyes. They cling so close to the leaves that not even a shadow gives away their presence. The glass frog's delicate body is almost transparent; through it, possible predators can see the leaf it's resting on.

A few insects actually cover themselves in pieces of their surroundings. Some species of caterpillars may stick bits of lichen (LIE-kuhn) onto stiff hairs

on their backs, and some grasshoppers and bugs fix stones onto their backs in the same way.

Some animals really are the same shape as lifeless objects. Certain caterpillars feed on leaves in broad daylight yet look like moist brown-and-white bird droppings. Bird-dropping spiders use a similar disguise,

A horned frog, or leaf frog, from the Malaysian rain forest is hard to spot among the dead leaves on the forest floor.

tucking their legs under their body to form the right shape.

Katydids and bush crickets are often shaped like foliage—some like fresh green leaves and others more like dead leaves. A few even have patterns of blemishes that look as if they have been eaten by insects or attacked by fungi.

Praying mantises often resemble clusters of dead leaves or even flower petals. Flower mantises keep quite still on matching flowers until an insect comes close enough to seize.

The petal-shaped legs and body of this Asian flower mantis make it look like an orchid. Insects trying to land on it are seized and eaten.

Confusing Patterns

Some of the most brightly colored birds and butterflies are actually camouflaged. Many predators search for the shape of the creatures they are hunting. In the bright colors of the sunlit patches of rain forest, dramatic color patterns can break up the outline of an animal so it doesn't look like anything familiar. The bold stripes and patterns of many colorful butterflies help disguise their shape when viewed from a distance.

Larger animals have to match background patterns on a different scale. Animals like hogs and deer must blend with the pattern of light and shade caused by beams of sunlight filtering through the leaves of the great trees above. Baby hogs and peccaries are spotted or striped, and so are many baby deer. Many large snakes have a dramatic pattern of all shades of brown and even orange. This breaks up their outline and helps them blend in with the pattern of light on the forest floor.

Butterflies and caterpillars have another trick. The most delicate part of their bodies are their heads. A caterpillar may have a "false head" at its tail end. If attacked by a bird, there is a 50 percent chance that only its tail will be harmed.

IN FOCUS

Changing Color

The chameleon (kuh-MEEL-yuhn) is famous for changing color to match its background. Tiny cells containing different colored pigments expand or contract, thus changing the color and pattern of the skin. Its eyes and parts of its skin sense the colors of its surroundings and send signals along nerves to its brain. The brain then orders the pigment cells to change size.

Check these out:
- Butterfly and Moth ● Cat ● Chameleon
- Constrictor ● Deer ● Frog and Toad
- Grasshopper, Cricket, and Katydid

Canopy

The tropical rain forest is not just a single, uniform environment but rather several separate and distinct ecosystems. On the forest floor, life flourishes under the soil, on the soil, and hidden among the leaf litter. The ground vegetation and understory are the habitat of still more forms of life, while the trunks of the trees themselves provide a habitat for their own unique flora and fauna. However, by far the richest ecosystem within the rain forest is nearly 100 feet (30 m) above the ground in the canopy.

For scientists this is one of the most inaccessible parts of the forest and, until recently, the least studied. From the air the canopy appears as a dense, continuous carpet of leaves. From the ground the canopy forms an almost complete barrier to sunlight. It is difficult to tell where one tree ends and another begins as their branches interlock high above the forest floor.

Much of what scientists used to know about the canopy came from observation of trees that had been felled. The problem is that by the time the tree hits the ground, much of the animal life on it has either been scared away or is damaged or killed. Researchers still have a lot to learn about the forest canopy, and countless species of animals and plants are yet to be discovered there and described.

KEY FACTS

● The canopy is one of the richest and most diverse habitats in rain forests.

● Many of the animals living in the canopy rarely descend to the forest floor.

● Temperatures at the top of the canopy can soar above 100 degrees Fahrenheit (38 degrees Celsius).

An aerial view of the rain forest canopy in French Guiana. The canopy looks like a huge green carpet stretching for miles.

Studying the Canopy

Some scientists have established aerial rope walkways so they can move from place to place within the canopy. Others have erected huge cranes, the sort used to build skyscrapers. The crane can move small distances within the forest on railroad tracks. The arm of the crane can swing around 360 degrees within the chosen area, and two or three scientists can then be lowered down into the canopy from above to take measurements and collect specimens. It's a technique that works very well but still gives access only to a tiny fraction of the aerial habitat. It's also extremely expensive to build and install these systems.

The top of the canopy is the most exposed part of the rain forest, open to the full power of the sun. Temperatures can soar above 100 degrees Fahrenheit (38 degrees Celsius). The canopy also takes the full brunt of strong winds and heavy rains. One hundred feet (30 m) below, the forest floor is, by comparison, a sheltered environment, rarely exposed to sun or wind. By the time rain reaches the ground, it has bounced off countless leaves and branches and lost much of its initial force.

The branches of the trees interlock to form a three-dimensional mesh high above the ground. Any animals moving around up in the canopy never need to come down to the ground to move from tree to tree. Animals such as monkeys can move as fast through the canopy as they can along the ground. Some move faster as

Flowering trees really stand out in the rain forest canopy, like these in Costa Rica.

the branches of the trees to grow on as well. Epiphytes, plants that grow on plants, such as bromeliads (broe-MEE-lee-ads) and orchids, have developed roots that cling to the trees' branches and can absorb water and nutrients from the rain washing over them. In this lofty position their own leaves are exposed to the sun. The wind or flying insects, birds, and mammals pollinate their flowers, or their tiny seeds blow onto neighboring branches and germinate there. Some of these plants provide entire ecosystems in themselves.

At the center of each cluster of leaves of a bromeliad stands a teacup-sized well of water permanently filled by rain. A huge number of insects and other

they can swing from branch to branch.

The seasons in the tropical rain forests are not characterized by winters and summers but by dry and wet seasons (although it is never really dry in the rain forest). The plants and trees are not all synchronized to flower and bear fruit at the same time but tend to do so individually by species. When a canopy tree bursts into flower, it stands out against the sea of green, attracting animals from far and wide. Similarly when the tree bears fruits or seeds, wildlife from all over congregate on it to feast on the bounty. Because all the trees don't flower or bear fruit at the same time, a constant supply of food is available for the animals throughout the year. All they have to do is travel through the canopy to reach it, having picked up the smell of the fruit or flowers on the breeze above the trees.

Life in the Canopy

Not just animals have evolved to live in the rain forest canopy; many plants use

IN FOCUS

Bats Tenting Out

Pure white with a yellow or pinkish nose, white tent-building bats are not much bigger than a human thumb and live in small colonies of about a dozen. They chew along either side of the midrib of a large leaf, causing the leaf to flop down on either side of the midrib, forming a useful ridgepole tent. The bats sit hanging under their leafy tent during the day, protected from the rain. They return to this roost for several nights until the leaf starts to die. Then they make another tent in the same area. At night they head straight up into the canopy, where they search for tiny fruits. They are one of only two species of all-white bats in the world.

small animals have evolved to exploit these tiny aerial ponds. Tree frogs sit in the wells, waiting for insects to visit the plant and become their latest meal. Some species lay their eggs in the bromeliad's pool, and their tadpoles develop in the water, feeding on leaf debris that falls in. Thus the frogs have no reason to leave the canopy or descend to the ground. Some salamanders live in exactly the same way. They have feet that are modified into suckers, allowing them to scurry through the slippery leaves without threat of falling. Some invertebrates such as certain species of scorpions and spiders are found only in bromeliads that grow high in the canopy.

Some butterflies and moths lay their eggs on leaves high in the trees and feed on the flowers of the canopy—the butterflies by day, the moths by night. Some will never be seen on the forest floor. Bats fly over the canopy at night in search of food, such as fruit, nectar, flying insects, or even smaller animals like frogs.

Some larger animals also spend most of their time in the canopy. Sloths spend their lives hanging upside down from the branches and move slowly and deliberately through the trees. Their strong claws give them an excellent grip and can lock around a branch for extra safety.

Approximately once a week, the sloth will descend to the forest floor where it will deposit its droppings before climbing back up into the trees. Sloths rarely venture onto the ground, where they are extremely clumsy in their movements and thus are vulnerable to predators.

Monkeys are also common residents of the canopy. Spider and howler monkeys are supremely well adapted to life in the treetops where they search for fruit. They rarely descend to the forest floor but can sometimes be seen in the lower branches of the trees during their quest for food.

Sloths and monkeys must be constantly alert while exposed high in the canopy since there is at least one large predator that is on the lookout for them. Harpy eagles inhabit rain forests from Mexico south to northern Argentina. The eagles patrol above the canopy in search of sloths, monkeys, and other tree-dwelling mammals. They swoop down and seize their prey in their immensely strong talons and literally pull it off the branch. They nest only in the highest trees, where they can raise their chicks in safety.

The spider monkey uses its tail as a fifth limb when moving through the branches.

Check these out:
◐ Bat ● Bromeliad ◐ Eagle
◐ Ecosystem ● Emergent
● Epiphyte ◐ Frog and Toad
◐ Monkey ◐ Rain Forest
◐ Sloth ◐ Understory

Carbon is one of the few chemical elements that is found in all living things as well as in the ground, the oceans, and the atmosphere. Carbon is constantly circulating among living things and their environment. This process is called the carbon cycle, a cycle in which plants of the world's rain forests play a critical role.

KEY FACTS

● **Carbon dioxide is a "greenhouse gas"—it traps heat from the sun in the earth's atmosphere.**

● **About 2 billion tn. (1.8 billion metric tons) of carbon dioxide is released by burning trees cleared by deforestation.**

Where Is Carbon Found?

In all ecosystems carbon is constantly flowing between living things (plants, animals, and other organisms) and the nonliving parts of their ecosystems (soil, atmosphere, and water). Carbon is found in the air in the gas carbon dioxide (CO_2), which makes up about 0.04 percent of the atmosphere. It moves from the atmosphere and from water into plants during photosynthesis. Photosynthesis is a chemical reaction that plants use to make food. Green plants take carbon dioxide from the atmosphere and water and use energy from the sun to make sugar and oxygen. Carbon becomes part of the plants as they grow. Plants also give out some carbon dioxide as they respire.

Of all the world's ecosystems, the rain forests take in the most carbon from the atmosphere because of the incredible density of their plants and their year-round growth.

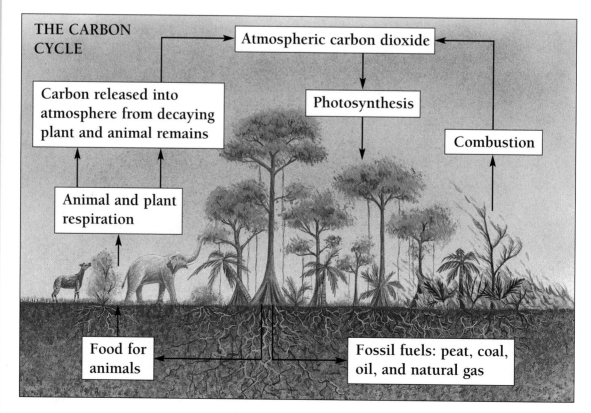

THE CARBON CYCLE

Atmospheric carbon dioxide

Carbon released into atmosphere from decaying plant and animal remains

Photosynthesis

Combustion

Animal and plant respiration

Food for animals

Fossil fuels: peat, coal, oil, and natural gas

Carbon moves from plants to animals through the food chain since animals eat plants or other plant-eating animals. As animals and plants die, they normally decompose, or rot. Decomposition releases carbon back into the atmosphere as carbon dioxide. Some dead animal and plant material is buried deep under layers of sediment where, over millions of years, it is transformed into rock or fossil fuels (such as coal, oil, and gas) by the intense heat and pressure. Burning wood and fossil fuels sends this "trapped" carbon back into the atmosphere, because carbon dioxide is one of the products of combustion.

Carbon also moves from living things into the air and into the water as animals breathe out, releasing carbon dioxide.

Unbalancing the Cycle

Through the natural processes of photosynthesis, decomposition, and respiration, the amount of carbon added to the atmosphere balances the amount taken out. Human activities, particularly deforestation and the burning of fossil fuels, which both add carbon dioxide to the atmosphere, disturb this natural balance in the carbon cycle.

Clearing the rain forests has a double effect. First, burning the vegetation releases extra carbon dioxide. Second, trees cannot grow again in the damaged soil, and so the carbon dioxide

remains in the earth's atmosphere.

Carbon dioxide is referred to as a "greenhouse gas," because it traps heat from the sun in the earth's atmosphere. This is called the greenhouse effect. As the amount of carbon dioxide in the atmosphere increases, more heat is trapped, which is now leading to global warming. Warming of this magnitude is altering climates throughout the world, affecting crop production, and causing sea levels to rise significantly.

IN FOCUS

Carbon Dioxide Increases

There is an amazing 700 billion tn. (640 billion metric tons) of carbon dioxide in the atmosphere. Annually about 20 billion tn. (18 billion metric tons) of carbon circulate through the world's rain forests. This amount decreases every year as deforestation continues and trees are destroyed. About 2 billion tn. (1.8 billion metric tons) of carbon dioxide are released by burning the trees cleared by deforestation.

Check these out:
- Climate and Weather ● Deforestation
- Food Web ● Global Warming
- Photosynthesis

There are three kinds of careers in the rain forest: as a research scientist; as someone who works to put the scientists' work into practice; and as someone who takes interested people on ecotours of the forest. All are part of the important job of conserving the rain forest.

KEY FACTS

● **There is plenty of work in the rain forest for all kinds of scientists.**

● **For scientists the main requirement is to be curious about rain forests.**

● **Non-scientists, such as park rangers and game wardens, also work in the rain forest.**

Scientific Careers

One of the main tasks of scientists working in the rain forest is to find out what is there and how organisms interact. Rain forest scientists also study the changes caused by natural forces and human activities. Because the rain forest is so complex, scientific jobs vary.

A botanist might work on taxonomy (documenting what plants grow in the rain forest), ecology (finding out why plants live where they do and how they interact with other plants and animals), or ethnobotany (studying how local peoples use rain forest plants). Zoologists study taxonomy and ecology, along with animal behavior. By reporting on animal population levels and the amount of hunting a particular population can support, their work can lead to improved wildlife management. Both botanists and zoologists also might work on genetics and phylogeny (how organisms are related to other species).

The rain forest is full of insects, providing plenty of work for this entomologist in Paraguay.

Hydrologists study catchment areas (the areas of ground from which rainfall runs into a particular river), water tables (the depth below ground at which water can be found), and the flow of rivers, including the effects of logging on streams and on the animals that live in them. The work of soil scientists, podologists, has shown how infertile rain forest soils are. Meteorologists find out how rain forests influence the weather, while anthropologists study the people that live in the rain forest.

Rangers and Wardens

Putting the scientists' discoveries into practice requires many different kinds of jobs. Park rangers and managers work together to run the forest, both for its

A researcher measures felled trees before they are floated downriver to the sawmill.

farmers to make the best use of their own land to cause the least impact on the environment.

Not everybody who works in the rain forest needs scientific training. Cooks and mechanics, nurses and pilots are all needed in the rain forest. The main qualification is a love of the forest itself and a sense of the work's value.

own sake and for the public's. In some countries they have the same powers and responsibilities as police officers, able to warn people who are about to break the law and arrest those who do.

Game wardens control hunting and fishing. They enforce the rules designed by zoologists and botanists to minimize damage to the forest and its wildlife.

Rangers often have the job of teaching people about the rain forest. A new and growing branch of education is known as ecotourism, in which people take trips to wild and remote places so they can learn about animals and plants that live there.

Foresters and Farmers

Foresters use the knowledge gathered by botanists to grow and care for trees and also to help loggers to understand their impact on the forest.

Tree farmers use the findings of botanists to grow new trees, especially those which might be used in the timber industry. This could decrease the amount of logging in the rain forest by lessening the need to cut down old-growth forests.

Agriculturalists study different ways of using land to grow crops or to raise animals. They can then work with

IN FOCUS

Wildlife Provides a Living

Anton Dey lives in the village of Wailebet, on Batanta Island in Irian Jaya, New Guinea. In 1994 an ecotourism camp was built near the village, where visitors could stay to watch the rare birds of paradise for which the island is famous. Dey is the best tracker in the village; now he and his two sons earn a good living by showing people how to find the birds. Other villagers also earn money from the growing tourist trade.

Check these out:
- Exploration and Research   - Forestry
- National Park   - Poaching   - Tourism

Carnivore

Carnivores range from tiny insects preying on other insects to huge tigers stalking their prey. Some plants are even carnivorous, luring insects onto their leaves with sweet sap, then trapping them to digest at their leisure. Some carnivorous animals are at the very top of the food chain.

At the bottom of the food chain are plants. As they grow, trees and plants turn nutrients in the soil, along with water and sunlight, into leaves. Plant-eating animals munch away at the leaves, and each of these animals has its own set of predators. In this way nutrients are transferred from plants right through the food chain.

To be a successful predator, an animal needs powerful muscles to chase down and seize prey, as well as the ability to move swiftly and quietly. Excellent eyesight helps to spot prey before it is aware of the danger as well as to judge distances from prey accurately. Predators who are well camouflaged can sit and wait unseen for prey to come within range.

One essential feature of most predators is a good set of teeth to break up and swallow its prey. Carnivorous mammals such as shrews and bats have many small, needle-sharp teeth to deal with their primary prey—insects. They must eat large amounts of food to fuel their highly active lives. Other predators feed less frequently.

Crocodiles and caiman possess a jaw full of sharp teeth that are used to keep a tight grip on their prey, which includes slippery items such as fish and frogs. A large crocodile may only have to feed once a week but can go without food for several months. The South American caiman lizard feeds almost exclusively on snails that it crunches using its specialized, rounded teeth.

Large forest-living snakes such as the anaconda and pythons have rows of teeth facing backward to pull their prey in and

KEY FACTS

● The carnivores include some of the biggest animals in the rain forest.

● Carnivores usually hold a place near the top of the food chain.

● There are two kinds of carnivorous animals: one is the order of animals called Carnivora, while the other kind simply refers to meat-eating animals of any order.

Rain forest carnivores come in all shapes and sizes.

Army Ant

Anaconda

Chameleon

swallow them whole. It may be two weeks before they need to search for their next meal.

True Carnivores

A large number of the Carnivora order inhabit the tropical rain forests; some of them are the largest, flesh-eating animals there. Members of the Carnivora order have one thing, other than their taste for flesh, in common: they possess special "carnassial" teeth. They are all descended from a common ancestor that evolved specialized teeth for slicing through flesh. Many animals can be said to be carnivorous, but only those that possess these teeth are true members of the Carnivora order.

The Cat Family

Cats are a remarkably uniform group of carnivores. All cats,

A Crocodile's Smile

Crocodiles and alligators are constantly replacing their teeth. They get worn down or even broken or lost when the reptile tackles large prey. If the crocodile's teeth could not be replaced, it would be a disaster for the crocodile to lose too many. New teeth form underneath the old ones, which are eventually pushed out if they are not lost when feeding. An adult crocodile may have replaced all its teeth several times during its 70-year life span.

Sun Bear

Jaguar

Spectacled Caiman

85

except the cheetah, have retractile claws, which means they keep them covered until they are required for hunting or climbing. This keeps their claws sharp.

Tigers inhabit the tropical rain forests of India and Southeast Asia. The largest member of the cat family, the tiger is a powerful hunter. Its hind limbs are longer than its forelimbs, an adaptation used for leaping out at its prey. Its stripes and markings give the tiger effective camouflage in the dappled forest light.

Tigers catch a wide variety of animals. They have been known to kill water buffalo and even young elephants. They will also take domestic stock such as cattle and goats, and, occasionally, humans. The tiger is an endangered species throughout its range.

The biggest cats in the Americas, jaguars inhabit tropical rain forests from Central America to South America, with their cousins the pumas preferring dense

A bushdog with her young. Very little is known about these animals.

forests around rivers and swamps. They can both climb and swim well and will not hesitate to enter water in pursuit of prey. Jaguars will eat just about anything, from frogs and fish to capybara and caiman, but are particularly fond of turtles and tortoises.

The jaguarundi is often called the weasel cat. It's an agile climber and emerges in the evening to prowl through the branches in search of roosting birds and small mammals. Its small head and elongated body allow the jaguarundi to explore small tree hollows in search of prey. It readily takes to the water to pursue frogs and fish.

Dog Family

Dogs vary in size from the tiny desert-living fennec fox to the forest-dwelling wolf. All have nonretractile claws and are well adapted for long-distance running. Some are solitary while others live in well-organized packs.

The gray fox is found in a wide variety of habitats but is particularly at home in tropical rain forests. Its range extends from Canada to Venezuela, including the rain forests of Mexico and Central America. Although foxes are not ideally designed for an arboreal way of life, the gray fox is an agile climber, hence its other name of tree fox. It spends the day curled up in the fork of a tree and explores the forest at night in search of small mammals, insects, and birds.

Bushdogs range over most of Brazil and northward into Panama. Very little, however, is known about them because of their elusive nature. Bushdogs do not look much like dogs; they are small, squat animals with wide heads and small, round ears, stubby legs, and short tails. It appears that they can live in packs of up to ten animals that hunt together. Because they hunt in packs, they can tackle prey much larger than themselves, such as capybaras.

Raccoon Family

Members of the raccoon family look like they are a combination of weasel and bear, but they are a distinct group in and of themselves. All members are omnivores, feeding on both plants and animals.

Coatis (kuh-WAH-tees) are curious-looking animals that inhabit the rain forests of Central and South America. They are about the size of large domestic cats but with longer, ringed tails, small ears, and long, upturned snouts. Coatis have strong forelimbs and claws for digging and breaking open rotten wood. Excellent climbers with an acute sense of smell, they search the trees for their prey, mainly insects, small animals, and ripe fruit. They tear open ant and termite nests to feed on the insects and dig into the soil to reach worms and grubs.

Civet Family

Civets (SIH-vuhts) are native to Africa and Asia. Mainly terrestrial mammals, they live in burrows abandoned by other animals. They have five fingers and five toes, each ending with a semiretractile, sharp claw. Most species are nocturnal and omnivorous. They feed on fruit as well as insects, worms, small reptiles, and mammals. They are best known for secreting a strong-smelling liquid known as musk. The palm civet inhabits the forests of Asia, where it hunts small mammals such as rats and mice as well as the occasional bird and reptile.

Bear Family

Bears tend to be massive, short-legged animals with nonretractile claws. Most are omnivores, eating both plants and animals. Many bears both climb and swim well.

In Asia the Malaysian sun bear inhabits the forests of Malaya, Borneo, and Sumatra. It is an adept climber and builds itself a nest up in the trees. This is an omnivorous species, supplementing its diet of flesh with fruit, nuts, berries, and honey.

IN FOCUS

A Spectacled Bear

The only bear in the rain forests of South America is the spectacled bear. Despite being a member of the Carnivora order, it is almost exclusively a plant eater. It is a small bear, about 3 ft. (90 cm) tall at its shoulders. The heaviest male can weigh up to 290 lbs. (130 kg). The white markings on this bear's face vary enormously from animal to animal. In fact no two animals have the same markings. With most bears, the white markings look like a pair of spectacles, giving the bear its name. Spectacled bears live in the rain forests of Colombia, Venezuela, Ecuador, Peru, and Bolivia. They are endangered due to habitat loss.

Check these out:
- Bear ● Cat ● Civet ● Cobra
- Constrictor ● Crocodile and Caiman
- Ecology ● Food Web ● Jaguar
- Mammal ● Snake ● Tiger

Although rain forests support huge varieties of animal and plant life, the soil itself is very poor in nutrients. Some plants have found a novel way of gaining the extra nutrients they need: trapping and digesting animals. Special plant juices digest the prey's body, which provides valuable nutrients. Plants have several ways of catching insects and other small creatures.

KEY FACTS

● **Some plants catch and eat animals to get extra nutrients.**

● **When an insect lands on a sundew, the part of the leaf it touches sends a tiny electrical signal that tells the tentacles to start curling toward the prey.**

● **Some pitcher plants of Asia produce pitchers big enough to trap birds and small mammals.**

Death by Drowning

The pitcher plants of the tropical rain forests have special urn-shaped leaves. In the bottom of each urn, or "pitcher," is a liquid. The plant may produce the liquid, or it may be rain that has trickled in. The plant lures insects with sweet-smelling nectar around the rim of the pitcher. Any insect that falls into the pitcher will drown. Some pitchers are lined with hairs that point backward into the pitcher so insects cannot climb out. Others are covered with loose, waxy plates that cling to the insects' feet so they slide in.

Many pitcher plants climb up the trunks and branches of rain forest trees, while others seem to grow straight out of the ground. This is because they are borne on creeping stems. Others produce pitchers at the end of long curling stalks. Some have little hoods to prevent rain from falling in and diluting the plants' digestive juices.

Some pitchers grow to a very large size; the rajah pitcher of Southeast Asia produces pitchers nearly 1 foot (30 cm) long. Each pitcher can hold up to 7 pints (over 3 l) of fluid. This pitcher plant is said to be

The half-open lid over this pitcher plant prevents rain from falling into it and diluting the plant's digestive juices.

able to digest small mice as well as insects and scorpions.

A few animals use pitcher plants for their own purposes. Small spiders may spin webs across the mouth of the pitcher to catch insects as they fall in. There is even a mosquito that lays its eggs in the water of pitchers. Its grubs can survive in the digestive fluid at the bottom and eat insect parts that are too tough for the pitcher. Little red-and-black crabs live in a plant called the phial pitcher.

The yellow trumpet of South America provides a home for small, green frogs. The frogs wait just below the mouth of the pitcher to catch insects attracted to the nectar around its rim. However, sometimes the frogs too fall into the pitcher and drown.

Sucked In

Bladderwort flowers on slender stalks rise out of the water of a rain forest pool. In the water below, the bladderwort's stems are covered with tiny bags called bladders. At the mouth of each bladder is a tiny trapdoor bearing very sensitive hairs. When a passing water creature touches these hairs, the mouth of the bladder opens suddenly. Water rushes in and the little animal is sucked in with it. The door snaps shut. The plant then pumps the water out of the bladder, and in fifteen minutes or so, it has reset the trap.

With 245 species, bladderworts thrive all over the world. Some bladderworts live in the small pools inside the bromeliads that grow on the branches of the great rain forest trees.

Living Flypaper

Bog violets are small plants that appear harmless. However, their leaves are covered in a sticky glue that entangles any insect that lands on them. The more the insect struggles, the more it spreads the glue over its feet and legs. Once the plant has caught its dinner, it makes sure of keeping it by rolling the edges of the leaf inward to enclose the insect.

IN FOCUS

Sticky Traps

Sundews have sticky tentacles on their leaves, each coated in a powerful glue that glistens like nectar. Insects landing on the leaf stick to the glue, and more and more tentacles curl over to trap the insect. The leaves produce digestive juices as well as glue. In just three minutes, the leaf wraps itself around the insect and starts to digest its meal. This amazing feat actually involves growth; one side of the tentacle grows faster than the other, so it curves.

Check these out:
● Nutrient Cycle ● Plant

Cat

Cats are found in all tropical rain forests of the world except those of Australia and New Guinea. The puma lives in the temperate rain forests of western North America as well as those of tropical Central and South America. The larger rain forest cats—tigers, jaguars, leopards, and pumas—are at the top of the food chain, but cats of all sizes are almost exclusively carnivorous, catching and eating live prey.

Out Hunting

Although cats have a keen sense of smell, they also use sight and sound to detect their prey. Cats have good binocular vision that enables them to notice movement and judge distances very accurately. Many cats, especially the smaller species, do much of their hunting at night. A reflective layer at the back of the eye helps them see in dim light. Their hearing is also extremely acute; large outer ears help to locate the direction of sound as well as funneling faint sounds into the inner ear.

Cats hunt by stealth, relying on their superb camouflage and an ability to creep quietly up to their intended victim. When close enough, the cats sprint forward or pounce. On the run, they use their forepaws, with claws extended, to bring down prey. Tigers and the other large cats often leap onto the back of a big animal or knock over and hold down a smaller victim such as a rodent with their paws.

Once caught, the prey is swiftly killed by bites to the back of the neck, cutting the spinal cord.

This fishing cat from India uses both its front paws, with claws outstretched, to catch a slippery fish in shallow water.

Jaguars often hunt near water, where they will catch and eat turtles and anacondas, as well as other mammals, such as tapirs.

pieces. Cats cannot grind up their food with their teeth. They eat slowly and, to avoid interruption, will drag their catch to a secluded place where they can eat in peace. They will often hide something that is too big to eat in one meal so they can return later to finish it.

Tigers, leopards, jaguars, and pumas often kill larger prey by biting its throat closed until it suffocates. Killing the prey quickly is important, for the struggles of the victim might injure the cat.

Special Teeth

A cat's teeth are specialized for killing prey and cutting its flesh into pieces small enough to swallow. Compared to other carnivores, such as dogs and bears, cats have short muzzles that allow a very powerful bite. The front teeth, or incisors, hold prey and pluck out feathers or fur. The large, pointed canine teeth act as daggers, stabbing deep into prey to kill it. A cat's cheek teeth have sharp edges. As it closes its mouth, the upper and lower cheek teeth meet like scissors' blades, slicing through flesh.

Cats of all species have tongues with rough, rasplike surfaces that help in eating and in keeping their fur clean. They also use their tongues to move their food as they chew, turning their heads to one side or the other as they bite the food into

Camouflage and Communication

The striped coat of a tiger or the spots of a leopard may look very distinctive in a zoo, but in a rain forest, these patterns are an effective camouflage. Stripes and spots mimic the patterns of light and shade on the forest floor or among the foliage, so a cat simply blends in with its background. Dramatic patterns and colors also draw attention away from the outline of the cat so that it is harder for prey, or a larger predator, to see it.

IN FOCUS

Retractile Claws

Cats have five toes on their front legs and four on their hind legs. Each toe has a claw that is concealed in a sheath when the cat is resting or walking. This keeps the claws sharp so they are always in prime condition to catch prey, climb trees, or protect the cat against attack. The cat extends its claws by contracting muscles in its legs that pull tendons attached to the toe bone that supports each claw.

Iriomote Cat

This medium-sized cat was only discovered in 1967. It lives on Iriomote, one of the Ryukyu Islands at the southernmost end of Japan. The Iriomote cat is buff brown and spotted with dark lines along its back. Although protected, it is still endangered as the amount of subtropical rain forest on its tiny island dwindles.

Just like domestic cats, rain forest species make a wide variety of noises to communicate with each other. Only the large cats are able to roar, but all cats growl—and all can purr when contented. Smaller cats spit or hiss to express anger or fear and, instead of roaring, will make yowling noises.

Large Rain Forest Cats

Tigers stalk the rain forests of India and Malaysia. An adult male holds a huge territory of up to 250 square miles (650 km²), in which there may be a number of female tigers. Male tigers live mostly solitary lives, associating with a female to mate and then perhaps to spend some time in a family group. Females are also solitary except when they have dependent cubs.

Tigers hunt in the cooler hours of evening and early morning, preying on deer, tapirs, wild pigs, and even buffalo. In the heat of the day, tigers keep cool in caves or by lying in shallow water.

The largest cat in African rain forests is the leopard, while in South America it's the jaguar. These are similar in

The jaguarundi often lives close to villages, where it helps to control the numbers of rats and mice, although it will also steal poultry if it gets the chance.

appearance, with rosettes of markings on a pale coat, but the jaguar has shorter legs and is much heavier. Both jaguars and leopards may also be all black and are often called panthers. Top-of-the-food-chain predators, these large cats are naturally rare as they require larger numbers of prey to survive.

Females usually give birth to litters of two or three cubs, although as many as six may be born. The female chooses a secluded, sheltered spot to give birth, and the kittens remain in this den until about one month old, when they start to follow their mother around. They usually stay with her until they are two years old.

Small Rain Forest Cats

The medium-sized and small rain forest cats are very agile, and many climb high into the rain forest canopy. As they move from branch to branch, their long tails

help them keep their balance; their sharp claws grip onto tree bark and branches. Some, such as the margay of Central and South America, the African golden cat, and the clouded leopard and marbled cat of Malaysia, spend most of their lives up among the branches, where they hunt and catch small mammals, lizards, and birds.

Others spend most of their time on the ground. The jaguarundi of Central and South America is a reddish brown, unspotted cat that is sometimes known as the "weasel cat" because of its short legs and long, slender body. It lives and hunts on the forest floor. The flat-headed cat of Malaysia and the fishing cat of India probably spend much of their time on the ground. The fishing cat catches and eats its food in or near the water; its diet includes crustaceans, frogs, and waterfowl. The flat-headed cat is reputed to include fruit in its diet, as well as frogs, birds, and small mammals.

The margay has a long tail to counterbalance its body as it leaps. It can also run down tree trunks headfirst.

Like their larger relatives, the smaller cats are mostly solitary animals, though they may spend some time together as a pair or family group. Females give birth in hollow logs, tree holes, or sheltered caves. Female cats carry their young by picking them up by the scruff of the neck. Young kittens are especially at risk from larger predators, including birds of prey.

Scientists know little about the life histories of many of the smaller cats. Most are rare, especially those such as the ocelot, margay, and clouded leopard, which have been hunted for their fur. They are all wary and secretive, silently moving away long before people see them.

Check these out:
● Camouflage   ● Carnivore   ● Civet
● Food Web   ● Jaguar   ● Mammal   ● Tiger

Cattle Ranching

Cattle ranching is the rearing of cattle in wide open pastures, as opposed to cattle farming, where they are confined to small fields. It began on the prairies of North America and the pampas and other natural grasslands in South America. When ranching spread to cleared forest land, it became a real threat.

Cattle ranching is a continuing threat to rain forests, particularly in Brazil but also in other South and Central American rain forest countries such as Colombia, Honduras, Guatemala, and Costa Rica. Because the soil is lacking in nutrients, rain forest land does not support the steady growth of grass that ranching needs.

Clearing ground that ends up being used as cattle pasture is the reason for about 70 percent of the destruction of the Amazon rain forest today. The idea of using rain forest land for ranching came from a failed experiment in which the Brazilian government tried to solve its problems with its growing human population. To reduce overcrowding in cities, the Brazilian authorities decided in the 1980s and 1990s to resettle large numbers of people in the Amazon River Basin, giving them land to clear on which they could grow crops. The settlers cut down and burned the forest, clearing ground that they could plant.

Cattle hands in Brazil. The work does not pay well, and it is wasteful of forest land, but at least these herdsmen have jobs.

94

Raging Fires

To encourage grass to grow, farmers use the ancient technique of burning, which often brings on a fresh growth of grass if it is done just before the rains. Sometimes the fires can spread out of control so that even more forest is destroyed. Similar fires, to clear land for farming and encourage grass for cattle ranching, caused a major ecological disaster in Indonesia in 1998.

Brazilian government decided to cut out the subsistence-farming stage of the process. Between 1980 and 1990, it paid a billion U.S. dollars to encourage cattle ranching in the Amazon. Even though the yield of beef is only one-twelfth of what can be produced on good pasture elsewhere, ranching provides jobs and brings in money.

There was an outcry among conservationists at the damage being done to Brazil's environment. Demonstrations and lawsuits left the Brazilian government in no doubt about the outrage of many around the world over the clearing of the rain forest. In 1991 the rate of clearing fell by 20 percent for the third year in a row, although at least 4,250 square miles (11,000 km²) of forest were cleared that year. However, this decrease was due more to a downswing in the Brazilian economy than to a change of heart on the part of the government. Since then, the Brazilian government has published figures designed to suggest that the rate of clearing is falling, but at least two large resettlement projects are still going on in the Amazon Basin.

At first the government's plan seemed to work, but it neglected to take into account numerous problems. Weeds and insect pests soon infested the thin soil exposed by removing the trees. In a short time, the infested soil became infertile. Another problem for the settlers was the fierce hostility of the local forest people, who resented having their tribal land taken from them, especially when they saw the way the newcomers mistreated the land.

The settlers gave up and went back to the cities. That was when large-scale ranching by outsiders began. The abandoned land was bought up, mostly by U.S. companies, and used as cattle pasture to supply the North American market with cheap beef to make hamburgers. The

Check these out:
- Central America   ● Deforestation
- Exploitation   ● Forest Fire
- Human Interference   ● South America

Rain forest caves are spectacular places. While most caves open out into sunshine that illuminates the mouth of the cave, those in the rain forest are surrounded by the green gloom of the forest, making their interiors darker. Caves vary in size from not much bigger than a garbage can to enormous caverns that could swallow a football stadium. They often teem with life; some animals use the cave as a place to sleep, others to escape the heat of the forest, and some live in the cave and nowhere else.

Rain forest caves provide a remarkably constant environment, permanently dark, with a temperature and humidity that remain the same whatever is happening in the forest outside. Fungi (FUN-jie) thrive under these conditions but no plants can grow.

Bats spend the day roosting on the cave walls and ceilings. Thousands, even tens of thousands, may have used the cave for countless generations. They emerge from the cave at dusk to feed on insects or fruit (depending on the species) and return around dawn to sleep. As they sleep, a constant shower of bat droppings rains down onto the ground.

Cockroaches move around in the dark, feeding on fungi, animal remains, and the mountains of animal droppings that build up on the cave floor. Cave crickets scurry over the walls. Their eyes are useless in the dim light, so they rely on their long, sensitive antennae, which they wave around in all directions.

Niah cave in Sarawak, Borneo. Rain forest caves are home to a variety of animal life.

Large, predatory whip scorpions hunt both the crickets and cockroaches. The whip scorpions track down their prey by sensing the vibrations the prey makes as it moves; they seize their prey with a pair of enormous, spiky appendages.

Some cave swiftlets nest in large caves in Borneo. These birds construct tiny slinglike nests high up on the cave walls, nests made up almost entirely of the birds' own saliva.

Check these out:
● Bat ● Cockroach ● Fungus
● Nest and Nest Building
● Nocturnal Animal ● Scorpion

Many different species of centipedes scurry through the rain forest. Some are quite small and easily overlooked in the leaf litter; others are large, active predators.

Despite these differences in size, all centipedes are similar in appearance. Their bodies are long and segmented; each segment normally has two pairs of limbs. The limbs end in sharp claws and give the centipede the ability to crawl up vertical surfaces—even upside down on the underside of horizontal surfaces. Large powerful jaws extend from the head end, and its front pair of limbs are modified to form hollow claws that inject poison into its prey.

All centipedes are hunters, feeding on insects, spiders, and small crustaceans. Some centipedes, such as the scolopendra, can grow to almost 10 inches (25 cm) in length. A creature this size is more than capable of killing and eating reptiles, amphibians, and small mammals. The bite of the largest rain forest centipede, including the scolopendra, rarely proves fatal to humans, but it is extremely painful and often leads to a trip to the hospital.

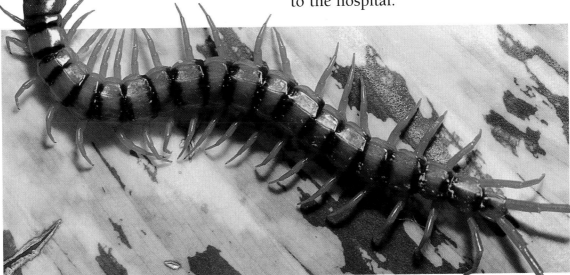

This scolopendra from west Malaysia is one of the world's largest centipedes.

A male centipede tracks down a female using its sense of smell. Many species exhibit a high degree of parental care. The female wraps herself around her eggs, cleans the eggs regularly, and protects them from predators. As the young centipedes grow, they shed their skins at regular intervals. This molting not only permits growth but enables the replacement of lost or damaged limbs and antennae.

Centipedes are nocturnal and prefer to inhabit damp environments. Rain forests are an ideal habitat for them; dozens of species are found living among the soil, leaf litter, roots, and tree trunks. They spend the day hiding in holes or under loose bark, emerging after dark to hunt. Most have extremely poor vision and rely on their sense of touch to navigate and hunt for food.

Check these out:
- Carnivore
- Forest Floor
- Insectivore
- Invertebrate

97

The narrow isthmus of land that forms a bridge between North and South America includes some of the most biologically rich environments on Earth. By far the richest are the rain forests that once covered almost the entire region.

The rain forests of Central America are home to more than 200 species of mammals, 800 species of birds, 200 species of reptiles, 150 species of amphibians, and hundreds of thousands of species of insects and other invertebrates. Around 9,000 species of plants have also been identified from the region so far.

Several small countries make up this strip of land: Nicaragua, Costa Rica, Panama, Guatemala, Belize, El Salvador, and Honduras. In general the geography of Central America follows a simple pattern, and a section through the isthmus anywhere from Guatemala to

KEY FACTS

● **The rain forests of Central America are among the most biologically diverse.**

● **Around 9,000 species of plants have been identified in Central America so far.**

● **The spread of ecotourism may yet save some of the region's rain forests.**

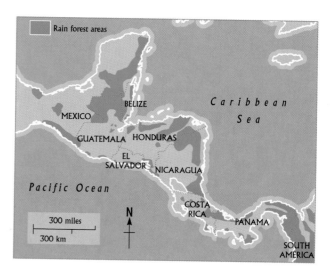

Panama exhibits the same characteristics. Once covered by tropical dry forest, the Pacific Coast is a hot, flat area that is now heavily farmed. Moving eastward inland, the land rises up to form a central chain of mountains, some reaching a height of about 9,900 feet (3,000 m). This is where most of Central America's volcanoes are found. Further east the elevation begins to drop on its way down to the Caribbean Sea.

Rain forests once covered virtually all of Central America, but today most have been cleared from the Pacific lowlands to provide land for agriculture. In the highlands many forests remain, except for the fertile valleys that have also been cleared for farming.

A view of a Costa Rican cloud forest.

Vast areas of rain forest still remain on the eastern side of the isthmus, although some were destroyed to make room for banana plantations. In places the rain forest remains wild and inaccessible, particularly in Nicaragua, Guatemala, Panama, and southern Honduras. In the far south, where Panama merges into Colombia, lies one of the most impenetrable jungles in the world, a mixture of hills, swamps, rivers, and thick, tropical rain forest, where heat and rain fill the air with a dense humidity.

Unfortunately much of Central America is riddled with economic and political instability, and little thought was given to conserving the rain forests in the past. Costa Rica and Belize now promote active conservation programs, realizing that there is more of a future in the conservation of the rain forests—more money for their economy through ecotourism and a healthier ecosystem— than in their destruction.

Cloud Forests of the Central Mountain Ranges

Cloud forests are aptly named; they are almost constantly shrouded by cool, moist clouds. The altitude, several thousand feet above sea level, means that these are relatively cool rain forests, with a unique flora and fauna. On some windswept ridges grow dwarfed forests where the trees are stunted to half their normal height and festooned in orchids, bromeliads, and other epiphytes.

On the lower slopes of the mountains from southern Mexico to Costa Rica lives one of the most beautiful and elusive birds in the world. The resplendent quetzal (ket-SAHL) is iridescent green with a scarlet chest. The males have incredibly long tail feathers—over 27 inches (70 cm)—that trail behind them as they fly. Other birds in this environment include the bare-necked umbrella bird and the three-wattled bellbird, whose single-note, loud territorial call echoes around the cloud forest.

On the forest floor live curious creatures called peripatus or velvet worms. They appear to be halfway between worms and arthropods. They live among the leaf litter, feeding on tiny crickets and other insects. Some species lay eggs

IN FOCUS

Extinct: The Golden Toad

On one of the high ridges of Costa Rica deep in the cloud forest at Monteverde, there once lived the unusual golden toad. The males lived up to their name and were a uniform bright golden-orange color. They were never common and had an incredibly restricted range, approximately 1/3 mi. by 3 mi. (.5 km by 5 km). Sadly none has been seen since the late 1980s despite frequent searches, and they are now considered to be extinct. Their disappearance may be attributed to a fungal infection or to changes in their habitat.

while others bear living young. A few species reach as much as 4 inches (10 cm) in length.

Rain Forests at Lower Altitudes

The rich rain forests that cover the eastern slopes of Central America are true tropical moist forests consisting of tall evergreen trees with multiple layers. The tallest canopy trees are around 130 feet (40 m) tall with long, slender trunks. Subcanopy trees are around 80 feet (25 m) tall; beneath these stand the shorter, understory trees. Epiphytic plants, such as bromeliads, orchids, mosses, and ferns, festoon many trees.

These forests teem with life from the soil to the very top of the canopy. Monkeys exploit every layer of the rain forest, hunting through the branches for leaves, fruit, and insects. Only rarely do they venture down onto the forest floor.

Bats fly through the understory and above the canopy. Some species feed exclusively on pollen and nectar, some on fruits, while others eat only winged insects. One species, the giant false vampire bat is a carnivore, eating frogs, lizards, small mammals,

and other bats. The true vampire bat feeds entirely on the blood of warm-blooded prey, such as chickens, horses, cattle—and sometimes humans.

Sloths inch their way through the trees to reach fresh leaves, while predatory cats patrol the forest floor and lower limbs of the trees. Jaguars feed on mammals, snakes, and birds, crushing turtles' shells with immensely powerful jaws. An agile climber, the smaller margay feeds on lizards, birds, and small mammals, hunting mainly at night. Slightly larger is the ocelot, which looks very similar to the margay. Because of its size, it can take slightly larger prey. It also hunts during the day as well as at night.

The forest floor is home to coatis, peccaries, and the largest mammal in these forests, the tapir, which spends almost as much time in rivers as it does on land. Its curious, long, flexible snout helps it sniff out the tastiest leaves. Only the jaguar can pose a threat to the tapir in the forest.

With such a richness in variety of flora and fauna and forests that stretch as far as the eye can see, it is not surprising that these tropical rain forests have a history of exploitation. In most cases this has been overexploitation, involving the wholesale destruction of entire forests for timber. Only the larger trees are used, but in reaching them, loggers irreparably damage the understory, which is then destroyed by the scorching sun in the absence of the protective canopy.

In many cases large areas of forests have been cleared to provide grazing land for cattle or farming land for bananas or other crops. The problem is that rain forest soil is quite shallow and not very fertile. It is suitable for growing only one thing— tropical rain forests. In the absence of the

IN FOCUS

Iguana Burgers?

It has been discovered that more meat can be produced by iguanas in existing forest than by cattle feeding in cleared areas. The iguanas are a natural occupant of the rain forest and rely on its diversity. Many Central Americans already relish iguana flesh, so they do not need to be persuaded to adapt to the new meat. Large numbers of iguanas are now being bred for release and harvesting projects in the rain forest.

Large areas of rain forest have been cleared to make way for banana plantations.

trees, whose roots hold down the dirt, the soil is quickly washed away and the land becomes useless.

Today some organizations are reclaiming these cleared areas by growing and planting trees and understory plants in an attempt to regenerate the forest. One such project is run by the Omere Wiki Foundation in Ecuador, which buys farmland that was once rain forest and replants it with trees and shrubs raised in large numbers in greenhouses. At present the foundation is working on a project to replant the El Chaco region.

In addition people are now trying to use products from the remaining rain forest without destroying it. It is only in the last 15 years that the Western world has discovered other treasures in the rain forests—pharmaceuticals. A huge variety of naturally occurring drug compounds that are useful to people are being discovered in both the plants and animals of the rain forests.

However, a good way of preserving the rain forest of Central America is to make parts of it accessible to everyone. Ecotourism is a major moneymaker for Central American countries, and it is growing fast. Tourists now flock to walk along trails through the forest, hoping to catch a glimpse of its magical fauna. This use of the forests makes them very valuable, but only if they remain in pristine condition. The tourism itself must be done in a sensitive way so as not to disturb the balance of tranquillity of this fragile ecosystem.

Check these out:
● Carnivore ● Cat ● Frog and Toad
● Iguana ● Plantation ● Rain Forest
● Reforestation ● Tapir ● Tourism

Chameleon

Chameleons (kuh-MEEL-yuhns) inhabit the rain forests of tropical Africa and Madagascar. It is among the strangest looking of all reptiles, with a long, prehensile tail that can wrap around a branch for extra grip and even support the lizard's weight. The chameleon's feet have evolved to form clawed mittens with three toes at one side and two on the other—the perfect design for walking hand over hand along a branch.

The chameleon's eyes are bizarre, to say the least. They are located at the end of cone-shaped turrets that can swivel around independently of each other. One eye can scan the surrounding branches for food, while the other can watch out for snakes or other predators. If an insect is spotted, both eyes are brought around to point forward, affording the lizard excellent binocular vision and the ability to judge distance very accurately.

The chameleon's tongue is as long as its head and body and ends in a swollen, sticky tip. The lizard can shoot out its tongue with pinpoint accuracy to pick off its prey and carry it to its mouth.

A chameleon catches a grasshopper with its tongue.

A crest or high casque adorns the head of many species, and some may have one, two, or even three horns on their snouts. Some even have flaps behind the head that can be erected. These ornaments are meant not only to impress other chameleons but to deter predators; as the chameleon raises these flaps, it also hisses or opens its mouth wide in a threatening display.

Perhaps the chameleon's most remarkable feature is its ability to change color; it's able to blend in perfectly with the rain forest foliage that surrounds it. This, coupled with the chameleon's extremely slow movements, makes it virtually impossible for both predator and prey to spot it among the branches. Color change is also used as a signal to other chameleons. Males can go dark, almost black, in the presence of other males; females can signal to males their readiness to mate by changing color.

Many species of chameleons lay small, leathery eggs, putting two or even three dozen in a hole dug in the leaf litter. The eggs can take over nine months to hatch. Certain species retain their eggs within their bodies and give birth to tiny, fully formed young. They are independent from the day they are born and start off life feeding on tiny fruit flies and mosquitoes.

Check these out: ● Camouflage ● Insectivore ● Lizard ● Reptile

Chimpanzee

Chimpanzees live in the tropical rain forests of Africa between Angola and the Niger River. The chimpanzee is genetically closer to humans than any other animal on Earth. In addition the chimpanzee has hearing and eyesight similar to human senses, while its sense of smell seems to be more highly developed. Chimpanzees appear to have little in the way of language, although captive animals can be taught to use and respond to human sign language. They do, however, communicate with each other extremely effectively by using facial expressions.

There are two species of chimpanzee; the common chimpanzee (Pan troglodytes) is the most familiar species, while scientists only recognized the smaller bonobo, or pygmy chimpanzee, in the 1920s. Both species live in loose groups of between ten and twenty (occasionally up to forty) animals, consisting mainly of females with young and some males. Except for the firm bonds between a mother and her young, there are no fixed bonds in the group; its size grows and diminishes as members leave and others return.

Within the group both the males and females are arranged in a social hierarchy. Age determines the social position among the males of the group. The older chimps are the most dominant, while the younger ones are subordinate to them. A male chimp gradually rises in status as he matures. He will reinforce this status by noisily charging about, waving twigs and drumming his feet against tree trunks.

Most arguments seem to revolve around older

KEY FACTS

● **There are two species of chimpanzee, not one as many people think. They are the common chimpanzee and the bonobo.**

● **Although they are primarily vegetarians, chimps do eat other animals, including other primates.**

● **Chimps exhibit a range of facial expressions similar to our own.**

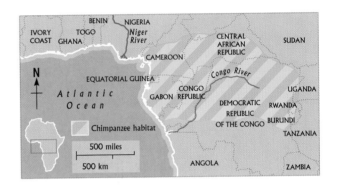

A group of chimpanzees examine an object. Chimpanzees are very curious by nature.

A bonobo, or pygmy chimpanzee, with young in the forests south of the Congo River. Although they are called pygmies they are not much smaller than other chimpanzees.

chimps failing to share food, but these displays of temper seldom lead to real violence within the group, only between rival groups. In fact chimpanzees are rather affectionate creatures. When they meet each other after being parted, they often hold hands, touch each other gently, and even kiss.

Grooming is an important part of the chimpanzee's social "glue." They will spend hours carefully sifting through each other's coats for sticky seeds and parasitic insects and seem to enjoy this contact with one another.

Family Life
Mother chimps are pregnant for seven and a half months. One offspring is the norm; twins are rare. Females seem to gain their experience of motherhood by watching older chimps with their offspring. The baby will be completely dependent on its

mother for at least two years. Baby chimps can move freely about the group and are constantly watching and learning from the behavior of other chimpanzees. By the age of six most young chimpanzees become independent and are responsible for finding all their own food.

Chimps spend the day foraging, feeding, and socializing and each night construct a fresh nest made of twigs and leaves in the trees. Adults normally sleep by themselves except for mothers, who usually share their nest with their youngest offspring.

Completely omnivorous, chimpanzees will eat almost anything. They look for food both on the ground and up in the trees. Though primarily vegetarian, chimps have now been shown to be much more carnivorous than was first thought. Some groups are active hunters, moving through the forest in well-organized groups in search of large prey. They have been known to attack and eat young deer and wild pigs as well as other primates. However, most of their diet consists of leaves and fruits. They are especially attracted to sweet fruits such as bananas and figs and often form raiding parties on banana plantations. An adult chimp can eat four dozen bananas in a single sitting.

Tool-Using Hunters
Chimpanzees are among the few animals that are known to use tools to solve some of their everyday problems. A chimp will place a hard-shelled nut on a large, flat stone and repeatedly strike it with another stone. Some of these stones appear to have been used for this purpose for several generations.

Some chimps use long, smooth sticks to obtain another food. They carefully lower

Body Language

One of the main ways in which a chimpanzee can express its feelings to another is by using facial expressions. Happiness and playfulness are expressed with a simple smile rather like our own but with only the bottom teeth showing. If both top and bottom teeth are bared, this is normally an expression of anger or fear. An expressionless face usually indicates that all is well with the world.

Aggression   Anxiety   Attention   Fear   Play

the stick, which is normally around 2 feet (61 cm) long, into a driver-ant nest. The ants immediately crawl up it, and the chimps scrape them off into their mouths before the ants have time to bite. Chimps catch and eat termites in a similar way.

A chimpanzee uses a stick to reach the ants he wants to eat. Chimps are among the few animals that can use tools to solve everyday problems.

Dangers for Chimpanzees

The main threat to all chimpanzees comes from the commercial logging and agriculture that results in the loss of their habitat. Commercial exploitation for the pet trade and for research laboratories has taken its toll but thankfully has almost ceased.

In recent years baby chimpanzees were stolen (usually by killing their mother) and smuggled to tourist areas in western Africa and southern Europe. Fortunately most of these orphans have been rounded up and are cared for in rehabilitation units, where it is hoped that at least some can be prepared for release back into the wild.

However, even in the wild, their future is by no means secure. They live in a part of Africa still suffering from the ravages of war. Many chimpanzees are killed for their meat (known as bush meat), and policing these areas for human hunters is almost impossible.

Check these out:
● Ape ● Carnivore ● Communication ● Gorilla ● Mammal ● Marmoset and Tamarin ● Monkey ● Orangutan ● Primate

Cicada

Cicadas (suh-KAE-duhs) belong to the large order of insects called the Homoptera, commonly known as bugs. There are about three thousand different kinds of cicadas, although they do not all live in the rain forests.

Cicadas have glassy wings and rather plump gray or brown bodies up to about 3 inches (75 mm) long. They feed by plunging needlelike beaks into tree trunks and branches and sucking out the sap. Their colors blend well with the bark, and the insects are not easy to find, even when they are singing. Large eyes alert them to nearby movements, and if a predator tries to get close to them, they either shuffle around to the other side of the trunk or branch or, with a harsh rustling of wings, fly rapidly away.

Cicadas are among the world's noisiest insects and can be heard for at least a quarter of a mile (400 m). Rain forests are full of their shrill calls by day and sometimes well into the night. The noise can be quite deafening.

Only male cicadas are responsible for the noise. A thin but very tough and springy patch of skin on each side of the male's body acts like a tiny drum skin. Muscles cause these skins to vibrate at high speed and produce the sounds. Some species produce monotonous calls that go on for several minutes without any change in pitch or volume. Others vary the pitch and volume of their calls. Each species has its own rhythm. Female cicadas recognize the call of their own species and fly to the trees where the males are singing. After mating the female cicadas lay their eggs in cracks in the bark.

Young cicadas are called nymphs, and each one spends several years sucking sap from roots in the soil. Big, spiny front legs enable it to tunnel through the soil to find fresh roots from time to time. The fully grown nymph leaves its underground home and climbs a tree trunk. After a short rest, its skin splits open, and the adult cicada struggles out. At first it is soft and green with crumpled wings, but the wings soon expand and the skin gradually darkens. Before long the new cicada is ready to fly. If it is a male, it soon adds its voice to the forest chorus.

A newly emerged adult cicada clings to its empty nymphal skin. Its wings are fully expanded, but not yet hard enough for flight.

Check these out:
- Bug
- Communication
- Insect

Civet

Five species of civet (SIH-vuht) inhabit the rain forests of Africa and Asia. In appearance the civet looks like a cross between a cat and a mongoose. Adults can weigh up to 22 pounds (10 kg) and measure over 3 feet (1 m) in total length, of which a third is tail.

Civets are found in a variety of habitats but prefer the dense cover of the rain forest. Nocturnal, they spend the day hidden in the abandoned burrows of other animals, emerging at night to hunt. Civets eat insects, frogs, snakes, birds, and small mammals. They will also eat birds' eggs and occasionally fruit. They can climb well using their sharp claws.

The common palm civet from Malaysia is mainly nocturnal.

The civet is essentially a solitary animal and avoids contact with other civets except when mating, which can take place at almost any time of year. The male tracks down a receptive female by the distinctive scent that she leaves in various places throughout her territory. The female has two or three young in a litter and may give birth twice a year. She normally gives birth in the safety of a burrow or amid dense vegetation.

The young are blind at first and open their eyes after about ten days. The mother suckles her offspring for about a month and then begins to supplement their diet with meat.

Human interest in the civet dates back well over two thousand years. Civets are a source of musk, a thick, brown, fatty secretion produced by both the male and female. When freshly collected, musk has an unpleasant odor but when diluted has an attractive smell and is used in some of the world's most expensive perfumes. However, the civets are not normally killed for their musk; instead they are caught alive and kept in captivity.

Civets produce musk constantly from special glands, or pods, under the tail. As long as the civets are kept alive, the musk can be harvested on a regular basis. Unfortunately the civets are not always kept under the best conditions and many die early from poor treatment.

Check these out:
● Carnivore ● Cat ● Mammal

Clear-cutting means removing all the trees from part of a forest. In plantations, where all the trees are the same age, it is an efficient way of harvesting the crop. In ancient, previously untouched forests, it is wasteful and destructive.

When forest dwellers need land for farming or building, they use hand tools to clear small areas, usually leaving large trees standing because they are hard to fell. These trees provide seeds from which the forest can grow back. Rotting, fallen trees and the standing stumps of dead trees provide homes for a huge variety of animals and plants.

KEY FACTS

● **No less than 87 percent of the temperate rain forests of the Pacific Northwest of the United States has been cleared.**

● **Scientists say that as much as 10 percent of the Amazon rain forest has now been cleared.**

Commercial Logging

When commercial logging companies come in, usually from overseas, they use modern machinery to clear the land completely. When clear-cutting is finished, no seeds for the future and no homes for other creatures remain. In some countries clear-cutting took place a long time ago. Over most of Europe, the forests were felled to create farmland in the Middle Ages, and in India they were cut and burned for firewood even earlier. Today forests are cleared not mainly for agriculture or for fuel but for wood, which is made into lumber, paper, and other products, and for cattle ranching. Ancient trees are cut down, usually in less-developed countries, and sold as timber in industrial countries, where the wood is very valuable.

In some countries, such as the Philippines, almost no rain forest is left. In others fragments remain that could be preserved. Paraguay was half covered in forest in 1940; by 1990 only one-third of

Clear-cutting leaves trees that grew up sheltered by their neighbors newly vulnerable to damage from wind and weather.

the country was still forested. Scientists say that as much as 10 percent of the Amazon rain forest has now been cleared—an area of about 38,600 square miles (98,500 km²), the size of Kentucky. Because of international protests about logging, Brazil will not release figures, and satellite images do not distinguish original forest from new plantations.

No less than 87 percent of the temperate rain forests of the Pacific Northwest of the United States has been cleared. When the first Europeans arrived in the early 1800s, the region was covered with huge, ancient forests. By 1900, using machinery, loggers could fell and process the tallest trees. Part of the cleared area became the city of Seattle, but most was left to become secondary forest. Some has been planted with new trees. The clearing continues more slowly today, partly because of protests by conservationists.

Worthless Land

Rain forest soil contains very few nutrients—75 to 90 percent of the nutrients are stored in the trees—so cleared forest is poor land, lacking fertility. In addition the roots of the trees hold the soil in place; when the trees are gone, rain will wash away the soil. Removing rain forest habitat makes countless animals and plants homeless. Forests create rainfall; when they are removed, the local climate becomes drier. Finally, logging roads allow more people into the forest so that poaching becomes more common.

Land that has been clear-cut is usually

Heroes No Longer

The early North American loggers were seen as heroes in their time. Working with axes and long, two-man saws that they called "misery whips," they felled gigantic trees of the temperate rain forests and dragged them out to sawmills. They were brave, daring, and very ingenious—and they could not believe that the trees would ever run out. However, even over 100 years ago, conservationists, such as President Teddy Roosevelt and Clifford Pinchot, chief of the Forest Service, warned against destruction of the rain forest soon after commercial logging began.

READY TO FALL, LUMBER SCENE, WASHINGTON.

used for a time for cattle ranching. When the cattle have eaten all the grass and trampled the soft forest soil, the area becomes a worthless wasteland.

Defenders of clear-cutting often say that it is like natural disasters, such as storms or fires, and that the forest will recover. But like clearings made by forest dwellers, natural disasters leave plenty of seed trees in the remaining forest. Clear-cut land would take several centuries to grow back to its former richness—if a seed source were nearby.

Check these out:

- Cattle Ranching
- Deforestation
- Exploitation
- Human Interference
- Logging
- Slash and Burn

Glossary

Arboreal: an animal that spends most of its life in the trees.

Binocular vision: the coordinated use of both eyes to judge with great accuracy the size of an object and its distance.

Biodiversity: the variety of different species of animals and plants in a particular area.

Catchment area: the area of land from which rainfall flows into a particular system of rivers.

Crop: a soft, baglike part of the digestive system where a bird stores food before it is crushed by the gizzard and digested in the stomach.

Deciduous: falling out or off at a certain time of year, such as the fall of leaves in autumn.

Decomposition: the process of decay that begins when animals and plants die.

Deforestation: the destruction of forest trees by felling or burning to create land for farming, ranching, mining, and towns.

Ecological niche: the unique attributes of a species that allow it to survive and reproduce under certain biological and environmental conditions.

Ecosystem: a group of plants and animals that interact with each other in an area (called their environment). A single tree and a whole forest are both ecosystems.

Epiphyte: a name given to any plant that grows on another without taking any food from it. Most epiphytes grow on trees.

Fauna: animal life.

Flora: plant life.

Gene: a tiny fragment of genetic material in the nucleus of a plant or animal cell. It controls one or more characteristics of the plant or animal.

Incubate: to keep eggs warm until they hatch.

Isthmus: a narrow fringe or strip of land.

Larva: the early stage of an insect's life. It may look completely different from the adult stage (e.g., a caterpillar is the larva of a butterfly).

Microbe: a microscopic organism, especially bacteria that cause disease.

Molt: when animals shed their skins in order to develop a stage further.

Nectaries: the parts of a flower that produce and store nectar to attract birds and insects.

Nucleus (*pl.* nuclei): a tiny structure inside all animal and plant cells. It controls what the cell does and contains genetic material.

Oxbow lake: a piece of landlocked river that is left behind when a river changes its course.

Parasite: an organism (plant or animal) that lives off another living organism without killing it.

Phylogeny: the evolutionary history of a plant or animal: what its ancestors were.

Poacher: a person who hunts or steals animals that are protected by law.

Prehensile: a limb that can grasp objects, such as a tail that can grip branches.

Proboscis: the name given to the slender tongue of a butterfly or moth, and also to the piercing beaks of some other insects.

Pupa: the stage in an insect's life cycle when the tissues of the larva (grub or caterpillar) are replaced by those of the adult. Pupae are usually encased in a hard covering or a silk cocoon.

Regurgitate: to bring up food from the stomach after being swallowed.

Reproductive system: that part of a plant or animal that is involved in the production of offspring.

Rosette: a circular pattern of markings arranged rather like the petals of a rose.

Stamen: the part of a flower that produces pollen.

Surface tension: the thin, skinlike coating on the surface of water when water meets air.

Terrestrial: an animal or plant that lives on land.

Understory: that part of the rain forest that lies beneath the canopy.

Index

112